A Philosophy
of Shame

A Philosophy of Shame

A Revolutionary Emotion

Frédéric Gros

Translated by Andy Bliss

VERSO

London • New York

This work was published with the help of the French
Ministry of Culture – Centre national du livre
Ouvrage publié avec le concours du Ministère français
chargé de la culture – Centre national du livre

This English-language edition first published by Verso 2025
Originally published as *La Honte est un sentiment révolutionnaire*
© Albin Mich 2021
Translation © Andy Bliss 2025
The manufacturer's authorised representative in the EU for product safety (GPSR) is
LOGOS EUROPE, 9 rue Nicolas Poussin, 17000, La Rochelle, France
Contact@logoseurope.eu

The moral rights of the author and translator have been asserted

1 3 5 7 9 10 8 6 4 2

Verso
UK: 6 Meard Street, London W1F 0EG
US: 207 32nd Street, New York, NY 10016
versobooks.com

Verso is the imprint of New Left Books

ISBN-13: 978-1-80429-415-4
ISBN-13: 978-1-80429-416-1 (UK EBK)
ISBN-13: 978-1-80429-417-8 (US EBK)

British Library Cataloguing in Publication Data
A catalogue record for this book is available from the British Library

Library of Congress Cataloging-in-Publication Data

Names: Gros, Frédéric, author. | Bliss, Andy, translator.
Title: A philosophy of shame : a revolutionary emotion / Frédéric Gros ;
  translated by Andy Bliss.
Other titles: Honte est un sentiment révolutionnaire. English
Description: English-language edition. | London ; New York : Verso, 2025. |
  This English-language edition first published by Verso 2025. Originally
  published as La Honte est un sentiment révolutionnaire © Albin Mich
  2021. Translation © Andy Bliss 2025. | Includes bibliographical
  references.
Identifiers: LCCN 2024054945 (print) | LCCN 2024054946 (ebook) | ISBN
  9781804294154 (hardback) | ISBN 9781804294178 (ebk)
Subjects: LCSH: Shame – Social aspects. | Shame – Political aspects.
Classification: LCC BF575.S45 G7613 2025 (print) | LCC BF575.S45 (ebook)
  | DDC 152.4/4 – dc23/eng/20250113
LC record available at https://lccn.loc.gov/2024054945
LC ebook record available at https://lccn.loc.gov/2024054946

Typeset in Fournier by MJ & N Gavan, Truro, Cornwall
Printed and bound by CPI (UK) Ltd, Croydon CR0 4YY

For Michel Gardette

Contents

Foreword

When I first spoke to a friend about my idea for a short book about shame, the response I got was 'What a strange idea. Guilt, okay – Dostoevsky, Kafka. But *shame?*'

Looking back, his reaction surprises me because I have come to realise that shame constitutes a deep experience; it is broader and more complex even than guilt and encompasses multiple moral, social, psychological and political dimensions. And I would also say that Kafka and Dostoevsky are actually all about shame.

In my own life, I reckon I have experienced shame more often than guilt, and in taking decisions have been more swayed more by the diktats of the former than the injunctions of the latter. I am reminded of the passage in Rousseau's *Confessions* concerning the theft of a ribbon. It was clearly a tough confession for the author – it is the first (and also the last) time he ever tells the story, as if he has decided to expose a wound and then cover it up again straight away (at least from the gaze of others). And his reticence is understandable, given that the incident involves him falsely accusing the cook – a young servant girl – of stealing. The prospects for a servant dismissed for theft back in that day and age do not bear thinking about.

It is worth retelling the story: An old pink and silver ribbon goes missing and Rousseau is found in possession of it. Flustered and stuttering (because he is indeed the thief), he accuses the young Marion of having given it to him. This comes as a surprise because the young woman has always been loyal and well behaved. They are cross-examined before the masters of the house, and the young Jean-Jacques repeats the accusation. Marion begins to sob while protesting her innocence. Rousseau sticks to his guns with 'diabolical audacity', clinging to the lie as if his salvation depended on it.

He would prefer eternal guilt or even death to losing face for one brief but cruel moment. The fear of shame wins out over everything else. The power of the story lies not in its depiction of a scene of shame but in its description of the terror in the heart of somebody who is absolutely desperate to avoid being stripped naked morally – a terror that instils a remarkable obstinacy in him.

> When afterwards I saw her in the flesh my heart was torn. But the presence of all those people prevailed over my repentance. I was not much afraid of punishment, I was only afraid of disgrace. But that I feared more than death, more than crime, more than anything in the world. I should have rejoiced if the earth had swallowed me up and stifled me in the abyss. But my invincible sense of shame prevailed over everything. It was my shame that made me impudent, and the more wickedly I behaved the bolder my fear of confession made me. I saw nothing but the horror of being found out, of being publicly proclaimed, to my face, as a thief, a liar, and a slanderer. Utter confusion robbed me of all other feeling.[1]

My friend's reaction actually served to encourage me. You could fill entire libraries with books about guilt, but rather fewer have been devoted to shame. That said, it turned out that there was a leading author on the subject – and a major book – in every field: Serge Tisseron in psychology, Vincent de Gaulejac in sociology, Didier Eribon in social philosophy, Claude Janin in psychoanalysis, Jean-Pierre Martin in literary criticism and Ruwen Ogien in philosophy.[2] I was coming late to the party, but I didn't let this put me off. Without necessarily revealing them, I could draw on my own experiences and also on those of writers who have struck a chord with me (James Baldwin, Annie Ernaux, Primo Levi, Simone Weil). I could also reference female figures who have suffered humiliation at the hands of men: Lucretia, Phaedra, Boule de Suif, Anna Karenina, the Daewoo factory workers in the François Bon story and so many others besides.[3]

Shame is the major emotion of our time, the signifier of new struggles. The battle cry is no longer injustice, arbitrary treatment or inequality, but shame.

January 2021, Paris, Rue Saint-Guillaume. Olivier Duhamel, the president of the prestigious Fondation Nationale des Sciences Politiques, is accused by his stepdaughter Camille Kouchner of sexually abusing her twin brother repeatedly in the late 1980s. It turns out that the then director of Sciences Po (whom Duhamel worked with) has been aware of these claims since 2019. In response to the scandal engulfing their institution, students organise demonstrations and publish an open letter titled 'Shame' demanding the director's resignation. (Duhamel resigns of his own accord once he learns that Kouchner is about to publish a book detailing the allegations.)

September 2020, Belarus. Thousands of demonstrators march

through the streets of Minsk chanting 'Shame on you' at the country's leader, Alexander Lukashenko.

February 2020, Paris, Salle Pleyel, forty-fifth Césars film award ceremony. When Roman Polanski wins the award for best director, Adèle Haenel storms out, shouting, 'What a disgrace, it's shameful!'

In January 2020, Jean Ziegler, the former UN Special Rapporteur on the right to food, proclaims after a visit to the Moria refugee camp on the island of Lesbos that it is the 'shame of Europe'.[4]

Along with these stories, a new vocabulary of shame has sprung up for fighting for new causes and expressing new sources of indignation; 'flight shame', for instance, references the cost of civil aviation for the planet.

Three contemporary injunctions seem to have risen to particular prominence.

'Stop being ashamed of yourself!'

This is a cry of rage and an expression of the desire to start living again in the face of the depressing form of shame that poisons your existence, completely undermines your trust in other people and takes all the pleasure out of life. It condemns the victim to painful silence and self-loathing, and it hampers resilience.[5] It is a shame fuelled by people who hate difference, by arrogant upstarts and by dumb macho types. It is the shame of discrimination and stigmatisation. The injunction is a call to liberate your voice and actively reappropriate your identity in order to unshackle yourself. This is where the self-esteem merchants and personal development coaches come in, purveying techniques for overcoming shame and accepting yourself as you are. The watchword is: Don't let anyone or anything stop you from being yourself. Love yourself and be proud of who you are (even though emotional wounds and trust issues are likely to endure, despite all the promises).

'People have no shame any more!'

This is a cry of indignation from the moralists, educators and vocational psychologists.[6] It's a constantly recurring complaint. Exhibitionism and shamelessness have become the new norm, whether at school, at work or in the street. There are no limits or scruples, no sense of personal boundaries. Social media feeds on shameless self-promotion, and uncivil and boorish behaviour is rife.

Shame is critically endangered these days. Rude, loutish and shameless behaviour is on the rise, whereas reserve, modesty, inhibition and scruples have gone out of fashion, not least at school. If there is a crisis in our schools, then it is, above all, to do with the lack of shame.[7]

We are urged to recover our sense of reserve and restraint and to keep certain things to ourselves. People dream not so much of a shame-based morality as a return to the ethics of antiquity, where shame (*aidos, pudor*) was a lever of political obedience, a social watchword and a part of people's inner make-up.

'The shame is yours, not ours!' or *'Shame on you!'*

This is also a cry of rage. It is aimed at those guilty of cruelty, rape or incest, as well as cynical politicians, corrupt business leaders and insolent billionaires. It is heard during demonstrations and public protest movements, and involves a whole dialectic of rage, sadness and contagious indignation, and a channelling of collective anger. Shame acts as the spark that ignites the dynamite.

❧

This book is a complement and sequel to *Disobey!*, in which I asked where courageous disobedience comes from, given our fears, our social conditioning and our natural inertia.[8] I was of course speaking in the political sense (revolts against unfair laws, the refusal to accept the world as it is, individual soul-searching, and so on), not about delinquency and incivility. Taking my lead from Hannah Arendt, I urged people to take personal responsibility, turn their gaze inward and live in keeping with their own principles. This solution held true intellectually, but it skipped over the grand and poignant motifs of revolt and understated the powerful role that the imagination can play in such struggles. And shame itself is reliant on the imagination – you need it if you're going to 'be ashamed of the world' and tell yourself that things could be different.[9] You need it when you are ashamed *for* someone else. This might be the humiliated and defeated party – it is *from that person's perspective* that you feel the unbearable suffering – but it might also be the brazen, humiliating party, who obliges us to be ashamed *on their behalf*, although they themselves feel no shame.[10]

Personally, I tend to take to people in whom I immediately spot a certain embarrassment, awkwardness and shyness – it is as if their lack of self-confidence will provide the glue for a solid friendship. And I would instinctively distrust somebody who told me they would never feel ashamed. Shame overwhelms me when I listen to the news from around the world, the declarations of prominent politicians and speeches by business leaders.

What gives us the strength to disobey, to refuse to resign ourselves to this sorry and seemingly inevitable state of affairs and to keep intact our capacity for revolt is, in Primo Levi's phrase, the 'shame of the world'. Shame is an amalgam of sadness and rage.

It cannot be outgrown, whatever the life coaches might claim, but it can be transformed into anger.

We do not leave episodes of shame behind – we work on them, elaborate on them, finesse them and sublimate them.[11] Sometimes we turn them into a lever, an accomplice or a useful resource. We wring them out and purify them to eliminate the destructive sadness and the self-loathing, retaining only the undiluted anger.

1
A Bad Reputation

There is a striking dinner scene in the John Cassavetes film *A Woman Under the Influence* (1974). Nick is a foreman on a building site with a dozen men working under him. It is a very male world of physical labour, sweat and banter, with rugged friendships growing out of the team spirit. He has had to work his team two nights in a row, and they are worn out. He rang his wife Mabel the night before to cancel a long-planned evening out with just the two of them (the mother-in-law having agreed to look after the children). Mabel is kind and loving but a bit 'crazy', in Nick's words – unpredictable and uncontrollable. He knows it, and so do his work buddies. When he invites them back to his for something to eat before they go home to sleep, he wonders what state he will find her in. It turns out she's still in bed after a rough night – unbeknown to him, in desperation she went out drinking on her own and ended up meeting some guy.

The sadness is clear to see. The workers are somewhat over-excited at the prospect of eating at the boss's place. Roused from her slumber, Mabel makes a huge dish of pasta and sits at the head of the table in front of all these men. This is when the first hint of awkwardness makes itself felt, as she keeps asking people their names as if seeing them for the first time. These stilted attempts at politeness assume a disturbing intensity on account of her odd manner, so much so that one of the guys ends up tipping his plate over onto the floor. There's a bit of embarrassment and some laughter, and they soldier on, with a couple of them bursting into song. Mabel gets up and starts complimenting another guy on his handsome face and his muscles, and now everybody starts shifting awkwardly in their seats until the master of the house finally yells: 'Sit your ass down!' A cry of anger and domination that brings the curtain down.

The guys all hunch over their plates, and a leaden silence falls over the proceedings. They finish up their food quickly and lose no time in taking their leave. Shame has descended like an opaque veil. It has gripped their throats, distorted their lips and given them a haunted look. No one feels at ease any more or knows where to look.

There is a distinction to be made between shame and guilt, which is also reflected in the language we use. The sense of guilt penetrates us personally, burrowing a tunnel of anxiety in the entity that we call the self. The web of distress weaves itself within us, clutching us in its icy grip. A friend commits suicide, and I replay the moments when I dithered over whether to go and see him or I cut short his moaning on the phone ('That's life for you!'). Everyone around me insists: 'Don't fall into that trap, it'll do you no good. You're not responsible.' I smile feebly back, but this standard advice does nothing to alleviate the bitter regret gnawing at me.

Shame is something else: a dense and pervasive substance, an objective state that does not depend on my own personal emotions or any subjective appreciation. It overwhelms me in one fell swoop. Whatever I may happen to think about it, objectively it is shame. It is not a matter of personal judgement, and there is no keeping one's distance. My sadness, if I feel any, is the product, the effect, the result of a situation that is *objectively* shameful.

The first type of shame we will look at involves family dishonour, public opprobrium and a deterioration of my social image, all linked to an *isolated* act (or omission), event or comment that automatically brings discredit on my clan. To illustrate this form of shame, we tend to look to the distant past or far-flung cultures. People will cite Corneille's *Le Cid*, recall scenes from *The Godfather* or discuss honour killings in Pakistan. Heroic morality and honour-based societies.

What anthropologists and historians define as 'honour-based societies' roughly encompass three types of community. There are the peoples (often Mediterranean) whose social structures are erected largely in parallel to public institutions (such as the Kabyle people, Andalusians, Sicilians). Then there are groups within established political societies, such as old aristocratic castes, some of which are now extinct and many of which have military associations (for example, knights, musketeers). And, finally, there are the Mafia clans organised around clandestine criminal activity.[1] I want to take a closer look at the inner workings of this archaic shame, drawing on the ethnographic literature but also on illustrations from the pages of fiction. The specific content of rituals and the concrete mechanisms will obviously vary from one age, community and country to another.

At the centre of it all is an act or a particular type of behaviour that constitutes an affront and sullies a family's honour. It may, for example, be an act committed by one or more outsiders against a member of the clan: a rape, a physical aggression, a theft, an insult or an insolent attitude. It may also be something done within the group by a relative or a friend: inappropriate or cowardly behaviour, forbidden sexual relations or an act of treachery. But, however many instances we might wish to enumerate, it is clear enough that the sexuality of women (*mother*, *wife*, *sister*) is the mainstay of the honour of the group – their sexual purity is the guarantor of it.[2] A simple sexual misdemeanour or an undignified scuffle is enough to tarnish a reputation and sully a family. There is now a stain on me, on my image, on us, on our name and on our honour. Shame has descended on us.

Corneille's characters include old soldiers and aristocrats who are proud of the family name and whose words and deeds are regimented by a code of conduct. In this world, the sources of offence are less often sexual. Among the soldiers, the triggers are mostly insolent remarks, acts of defiance, insults, offensive behaviour or bad jokes. Take Don Diègue, the glory-covered veteran from Spain in *Le Cid*. His arm trembling, he falters under the welter of insults from his younger rival, who is jealous of his royal promotion. His famous tirade ('Oh rage, oh despair …') spells out the disaster that has befallen him: all his great deeds abruptly cancelled out by a moment of weakness. His reputation has all of a sudden gone sour like old milk, and he is now nothing – stripped of his dignity and ruined. His honour was his invisible overcoat, and how can he now go out in public? No amount of philosophy lessons, friendly shoulders to cry on or sessions on the psychiatrist's couch are going to solve this problem. In allowing his rival to insult him with impunity, Don Diègue has contracted a debt of shame. Now he has to pay back that debt, unless he wants to 'die without vengeance or live in shame'. It is, ultimately, his son who will avenge him. In this instance, shame is not so much a question of psychology as an erosion of symbolic social capital.

This form of shame involving clan dishonour has four defining qualities: It is objective, tangible, collective and reversible.

Objective in that it is not a psychological issue that can be treated through therapy. The emotional dimension is secondary – the shame derives from an objective fall in social status. After I am insulted in public and I fail to retaliate when slapped, the issue is not what inner fragility or lack of assertiveness this reveals. The insults and the cowardly failure to react to the physical aggression automatically and objectively engender shame. Never mind how I feel, there is nothing I can do about it – I can say goodbye to my image and the honour of my family. They are tarnished, tainted, sullied. This type of shame is the result of a social mechanism, not individual psychology.

Tangible in that the shame is not a mere subjective impression, inner construction or private feeling. It is a substance that blackens, tarnishes, stains, defiles and darkens – a kind of viscous negativity that sticks to you. It is also a deliquescence, a liquefying of prestige. Social dignity is articulated in a double register: the economic and the biological. Honour is a family's wealth, its symbolic opulence. Honour is synonymous with the blood, health and energy of the group; it is the force that sustains each of its members, a capital that is constantly vulnerable to being debased, slashed to pieces, or whittled away by *affronts*. It is perceived of as a 'thing' to such an extent that it has been used as a guarantee – in the Middle Ages, a person of good birth could offer his honour as security when lending or borrowing money.[3] He was accepting in advance that he would be insulted, slandered, mocked and defamed if he breached the terms of the agreement. And it was by no means a sucker deal: Shame can ruin you, bleed you dry.

Collective in that this blood and this wealth do not belong to me *personally*. It is not *my* blood, *my* wealth, *my* honour, but those of a clan, a group, a whole family. These things course through me, nourish me and support me, and are a substantial part of me. If I'm insulted or assaulted, if my cousin behaves in a cowardly way or if my sister does not observe proprieties, it is the vital symbolic capital of our family that is diminished, and shame will duly descend on the group like a dark shroud.

But this shame is ultimately *reversible*. This is the most important characteristic of the shame of opprobrium and what gives it its archaic aura. It is a dialectical process: Shame is the negation of honour (one's primary asset); vengeance is the negation of this negation and hence the restoration of the lost honour. Intrinsic to the shame of dishonour is that it can be washed clean, erased, dissolved. The objective nature of this type of shame is what provokes the agony (once the affront has occurred, the repercussions are automatic and uncontainable), but it is also its redeeming feature. It can just as automatically be cancelled out and erased by observing age-old and meticulously defined procedures: One must *publicly* engineer a dramatic and finely calibrated riposte that balances things out – an act of revenge that reverses the original humiliation, whereupon the shame will disappear like a face drawn in the sand. The mechanisms for restoring one's honour vary. The most familiar, when offence has been given by another clan (interfamilial justice: *dikē*[4]), is vengeance.[5] One avenges the insult, the insolent remark, the aggression or the affront through a codified and carefully prepared riposte that publicly stages the cancelling out of the shame. This might take the form of a challenge to a duel, a settling of the scores in a particular way or a ritualised duplication of the offence. If it is a personal weakness that has been exposed to the public glare, the path to atonement generally obeys a certain logic. Somebody guilty of cowardice, for example, might redeem himself through a shining act of heroism that eclipses his former shame.

But when the terrible affront occurs within a family and involves the parents, the situation is different because you do not take revenge on close family members. Anthropologists have described other mechanisms for purging shame (intrafamilial justice: *themis*) such as exclusion, sacrifice, the repudiation of the person who is the source of opprobrium, the moral rejection of the traitor or the physical massacre of women guilty of sexual impropriety. In Balzac's 1830 novel *La Vendetta*, a beloved only daughter falls in love with a young man from an enemy clan with whom there is very bad blood; she is cast out by her parents and goes off to live with him. The documentary *A Girl in the River: The Price of Forgiveness* tells the true story of a young Pakistani woman called Saba who marries a young man from a lower social class – perfectly *legally* but against the wishes of her family – and is kidnapped, beaten, disfigured by a revolver bullet to the face and thrown into a river tied up in a sack.[6] Her marriage was deemed to have brought dishonour on the family. Over 1,000 women are killed every year in Pakistan for having 'shamed' their families. Closer to home, in Besançon, France, in August 2020, the family of a seventeen-year-old Bosnian girl beat her and shaved her head for seeing a young Christian Serbian whom she wanted to marry. The 'explanation' given for these barbaric acts was that the family could not have borne the shame that this unsuitable marriage would have entailed.

~

Then there is the story of Lord Jim in Conrad's eponymous novel.[7] Jim is a twenty-four-year-old sailor full of dreams of glory. He secures a berth as first mate on the *SS Patna*, an old steamship packed to the rafters with pilgrims bound for Mecca. One night, the ship hits some wreckage and an ominous sound is heard; an inspection of the rusty iron bulkhead reveals significant damage. The ship is already pitching forward and seems certain to sink, but there are only a paltry seven lifeboats for 800 passengers. Waking the passengers would trigger a panic and would, in any case, be futile; better to let them sleep and sink quietly to an inevitable death. Lord Jim strikes the pose of the stoic hero and proudly awaits the end, but suddenly hears voices telling him to jump: The captain and two crew members have lowered a boat into the sea. Before casting off, they call out to the silhouette of Lord Jim, whom they take to be the third engineer.

And all of a sudden, Lord Jim finds himself sprawled in the bottom of the lifeboat – clearly, *he must have jumped*. A second before, he was bracing for death like a hero, and now he is in the place of somebody else fleeing for his life in the company of three cowards. Between those two moments, there is a blank, a void. In the distance, the steamship appears to sink, and many hours later they are picked up by another boat. As soon as he is back on land, the captain declares a shipwreck, and it is only then that he learns the terrible truth: His ship in fact stayed afloat and was spotted by a French gunboat. The crew were missing but the passengers were safe and sound, if a little haggard. It is a miracle that the wreck did not sink, and who can predict a miracle? All that remains is shame and infamy. History's verdict alters: The four wretched survivors are, in fact, four ignoble deserters.

The captain and his accomplices flee, but a dignified Jim chooses to stand trial alone, which brings dishonour and the loss of his certificate to sail. He is the only one with the courage to let himself be judged publicly, and his name will become a byword for infamy. In every port of the Orient, people will tell the story of Jim, the sailor who abandoned to their fate 800 pilgrims aboard an old wreck of a ship. Why did he not flee like the others? In order to confront the enigma of that leap – that sudden and unpremeditated act which landed him and his heroic dreams in the bottom of a lifeboat. To invite the boundless contempt of others on himself. To drink down the cup of shame to the dregs.

The story articulates a shame devoid of any guilt. Jim has no deaths on his conscience; what he has done has harmed no one and nothing except for his image, his prestige and his reputation. For many years, he will try to flee his own shadow, his personal history. And in the end – it is the final scene of the novel – he will valiantly face up to death without flinching in a heroic act of atonement that washes him clean, *thereby preventing his shame from outliving him.*

2

Societies without Honour?

Clan-based shame arising out of the moral codes of long-established family structures has never been to the taste of philosophers. Beginning in the seventeenth century, they reconfigured it in order to disqualify it, placing the emphasis instead on individual psychology. Around a decade after *Le Cid*, Descartes wrote: 'Shame, on the other hand, is a kind of sadness based also on self-love, which comes from expecting to be blamed or being anxiously aware that one may be blamed.'[1] Some years later, Spinoza took a similar line in his *Short Treatise*:

> Shame is a certain kind of sorrow which arises in one when he happens to see that his conduct is despised by others ... For Glory and Shame are not only of no advantage ... but also ... they are pernicious and must be rejected.[2]

Classical-era moralists minimise the importance of shame. It is no longer a binding and ritualised social mechanism that can be disastrous for families, but a minor personal drama whereby an individual has to contend with the negative judgement of others. It is a rather lame 'sadness' arising out of narcissism, and the contagious, collective, ritual dimension disappears. Shame becomes a misplaced susceptibility (which cannot be completely ignored, as one nevertheless has to conform to the moral values of one's time). It is neither a symbolic debt to be repaid nor a vital capital to be replenished, but the petty affair of a diminished ego: Whatever are people going to think of me?

This diminishment reflects a cultural preference (though not, as it happens, on the part of Descartes or Spinoza) for another emotion that is considered more 'morally appropriate': guilt (or remorse or regret) arising from an abuse of my freedom.[3] It is clear enough what oppositions are at work here to the detriment of shame: interiority versus exteriority, depth versus superficiality, authenticity versus *doxa*, transcendent values versus social conventions. The influence of Christian morality and its over-insistence on guilt can be felt behind this conceptual contraction – Saint Augustine condemns Lucretia for committing suicide after being raped by one of her husband's comrades-in-arms, considering that she attaches too much importance to public opinion ('This matron, with the Roman love of glory in her veins, was seized with a proud dread').[4] This hypersensitivity to reputation in the shame ethics of families, this cult of public opinion, is contrasted with a morality that seeks to base itself upon an inner dignity and where the only thing that counts in the inner solitude of the self is the vertical relationship with one's conscience, not one's horizontal alignment with the opinions of others. True morality disdains popularity contests and comparing how many followers you have on social media.

Blame culture is not the only reason why the ethics of clan shame have somewhat faded into the background. The three pillars of

Western modernity, which have been identified and extensively analysed by an army of historical sociologists, have significantly contributed to discrediting this sensitivity to honour.[5] With the centralising of power came a rational obligation on subjects to obey the law (rather than observe a sacrosanct family code) as well as a state monopoly on justice. Channels of private vengeance were frowned upon and proscribed in favour of judicial resolutions sanctioned by a sovereign. Later on, liberalism placed the emphasis on individuals and their rights and freedoms, loosening the constraints of family and religious duty. And then capitalism came along and largely cast aside the symbolic import of debt, acknowledging only mercantile and monetary transactions: Everything can be bought, sold, negotiated, sold on and sold off.

It put an end to tragedy, heroines and avengers. All of Balzac can be reframed in this light, as a caustic depiction of the fading of sentiments of honour in the face of creeping commercialisation. It is the place where prostitution reigns supreme. On the threshold of the lair of the moneylender Gobseck, the symbol of the new civilisation in the eponymous Balzac novella, the message is 'Abandon all sense of shame all ye who enter here.' This is the doorway to the modern, liberal and capitalist state. Modernity constructs societies without honour. Communities are organised around a public body of laws (the state), commercial transactions (capitalism) and the interplay of individual freedoms (liberalism).

In the process, shame gets a makeover, becoming less clan-based and more bourgeois, less dramatic and more transactional, less ritual and more psychological. For a start, as we will see, a shame of being poor (or simply less rich) will emerge – something that is rare in honour cultures. Increasingly, poverty is felt to be less a matter of circumstance with vaguely Christian overtones than a sign of personal failure and thwarted ambition. Honour within families undergoes a transformation too and starts to go by the name of *respectability* and *normality*. The kernel is no longer the clan, the family line and name, or the web of connections through marriage, but the little bourgeois household – a married couple who are virtuous, hard-working and thrifty, who have children and own their property. Who get together for baptisms and birthdays, fret about the future of their offspring and are obsessed about their standard of living, the external signs of their virtue and the masturbatory habits of their children. The oedipal family, the nuclear family, the 'kangaroo family': an economic and sexual nucleus that was initially supervised by the priest but later appropriated by the doctor.[6] It has been a staple from the comedies of Molière right up to the French upheavals of May 1968, setting the boundaries between good and evil, right and wrong, virtue and vice, and normal and abnormal. What Michel Foucault sought to reveal and critique in his analysis of power and theory of norms is something that lies this side of public institutions, legal authorities, the judicial system and the law, namely the diffuse and irresistible power of *respectable* families who, in the name of the 'true' and the 'natural' and with the indulgent help of psychiatrists, have constructed the empire of the *normal*.

Normality is not a statistical pattern or a simple average, but a model of respectable behaviour. Normality is what passes for honourable in our honourless societies. The bourgeois family has obsessed about three major avatars of shame: the adulterous woman, the gay son and the masturbating child. It is this entity, more than Christianity, that has saturated sexuality with shame. Under the ancien régime, it defined the contours of infamy by exploiting a repressive tool offered to it by the monarchy: the infamous *lettres de cachet*.[7] Signed by the monarch, these letters were an arbitrary legal instrument that could be used to incarcerate (for a few weeks, months or even years) an individual who was causing a scandal through their 'inappropriate' behaviour. These people might include inveterate revellers, 'sodomites', women of easy virtue who invited too many suitors into their beds, spendthrift sons who were squandering the family fortune or blasphemers who publicly took the name of the Lord in vain. The *lettres de cachet* could be exploited by families concerned about a gay son or a flighty daughter in their midst, or simply worried that the local simpleton belting out bawdy songs in the street was dragging down the reputation of the neighbourhood.

In the popular imagination, these letters were used by despotic monarchs to eliminate their political enemies; in actual fact, they were more commonly used by 'respectable' families to rid them-selves of troublemakers and to get men and women locked up who, though they had not broken the law or caused any material damage, were nevertheless a source of *shame*. Family members compiled dossiers, reported disgraceful behaviour and painted a picture of a long-suffering family whose honour was at stake. After examining the dossier, a lieutenant of police would issue a letter with the royal seal that would result in the immediate incarceration of the offending party. They were not judged in a court according to the law of the land but imprisoned in the name of family respectability. Mirabeau was locked up at the instiga-tion of his father to stop him gambling away the family fortune, and the Marquis de Sade ended up in the Bastille on account of his mother-in-law.

This practice did not survive the French Revolution, but, for over a century, the family was the major locus of shame. It now had to find other extrajudicial means of dealing with those who sullied its reputation. Novel nineteenth-century approaches to treating mental illness overlaid intolerable behaviour with a system of vague pathological classifications, thereby taking care of deviants and abnormal types. Pigeonholed into psychiatric categories, they were interned in asylums, and madness became a 'shameful' illness.

One might have thought that hyper-modernity – combining the emancipation of moral attitudes from the 1970s onwards, with the insistent promotion of individual rights, the rise of libertarianism and the widespread adoption of sexual practices that had once been considered unmentionable – put the final nail in the coffin of the Victorian family and its shame-based values. But, with the development of social media (Facebook, X, Instagram, and so on), contemporary societies have added a new (digital) dimension to one's public image, which can now be quantified and fluctuate up and down like share values. Everyone on the internet puts themselves forward, tries to get noticed, brags, sells themselves, hones and embellishes their image, takes liberties and flaunts themselves.[8] For every post, there will be a generous helping (or paltry handful) of ratings, comments and likes that will comfort or irritate the author, and cause pain or pleasure.

People will claim that all this fun and games is but mere froth on the surface of reality – parallel universes in which people have friends by the hundreds and are always charming, funny, tanned, witty and photographed from the most flattering angle. But this virtual world is not quite the opposite of the real world, if, by reality, we mean what counts, produces effects, drives things forward and has a causal power. On that reckoning, the digital is *real*. Experts in addiction, for their part, highlight the similarities – in terms of releasing tensions, neuronal arousal and other physiological processes – between drug and social media

addiction. The digital projection of the self has become an addic-
tive substance. And social media functions through contagion:
content that is rapidly relayed and endlessly shared, thereby going
viral. Virtual = viral = real. It is in *viral-eality* that contemporary
shame emerges: social media accounts saturated with insults,
e-reputations ruined by e-bashing campaigns, an anonymous
deluge of gratuitous, sarcastic barbs that completely knock the
stuffing out of the internet user. You no longer dare look at your
account, and it feels like the entire world is conspiring against you.

One can identify certain characteristics of archaic shame here:
the objective nature of the opprobrium (an e-reputation is not a
subjective feeling – it is quantified by how many followers you
have) and the collapse of the victim's prestige. But the situation
is even crueller because our digital traces spread far and wide,
persist and lie in wait for us. All our shameful acts, major and
minor, are saved for eternity as data (relating to purchases, sites
visited, photographs, trips, selfies, contacts, videos), ready to
resurface and to catch us unawares. Our public image floats on
the web, forever susceptible to becoming a focus of hostility. In
the space of a few hours or even minutes, I can become the target
of a negative buzz relayed at a crazy speed. My downfall is a viral
affair, the denigration universal. Jon Ronson recounts some of
these falls from grace in a chilling book called *So You've Been
Publicly Shamed*.[9]

A life blown to bits, torn to shreds in the time it took to fly from
England to South Africa. Eleven hours from London to Cape
Town during which a young woman, unable to react, was subjected to a digital lynching that would cost her the respect of her
friends, her job and the love of her family. It all began with a joke
in poor taste she made on her Twitter account. Justine Sacco,

who had a handful of followers, had a habit of sharing tweets that were not always particularly funny and sometimes slightly alarming, which her digital friends would greet with polite indifference. On 20 December 2013, just before boarding her plane, she posted another of these bad-taste tweets: 'Going to Africa. Hope I don't get AIDS. Just kidding. I'm white!' A journalist called Sam Biddle spotted the tweet and shared it with his 15,000 followers, unleashing a tornado. While Justine was peacefully sleeping high above the clouds, a deluge of digital hatred was raining down on her account. Horrified anti-racists and understandably indignant leaders of AIDS associations reacted, as did the baying pack of casual hatemongers and cynical opportunists (including one Donald Trump). Her employer condemned her remarks on Twitter, and people were initially surprised at the silence of the interested party (who was still peacefully sleeping). The hashtag *#HasJustineLanded* was launched, and a photographer was dispatched to capture the moment when she turned her mobile back on. The moment she arrived in South Africa, horrified to see what she had brought upon herself, Justine deleted the tweet and her account. 'Sorry @JustineSacco, your tweet lives on forever,' warned one 'charitable' soul. In Cape Town, her dream holiday became a nightmare: The employees at the hotel she had booked threatened to strike if she was allowed to stay there, and her South African family shunned her. Between 20 December and the end of the month, the name Justine Sacco was googled over a million times. It had taken only a few hours to skin her alive, sack her and ruin her. A digital tsunami of hatred. The story is now a decade old, but you can still find her tweet if you google her name.

Digital shame survives you, and dying of it is not even a metaphor any more. People have committed suicide after being cyberbullied. Lives are ruined by viral revenge porn, and clips of people doing silly things resurface to destroy careers. But, in this instance, vengeance is not a possibility. There is no such thing as digital redemption. In the cloud, our shame is out of reach and inextinguishable.

3
Social Disdain

The shame of being poor is almost too abstract. You need to use words like *social outcast*, *bumpkin*, *bum* or *hillbilly* for the full sting of the judgement to be felt. Anyone from a humble background will be able to recall from personal experience those painful encounters with the world of money and material comfort, and with those cultural reference points (opera, free jazz, arthouse films) that are de rigueur in certain circles but petrify provincial types. You are ashamed of your own cultural baggage. You are ashamed of your dress or trousers, your shirt and your shoes. Only moments before, you found them very smart, but now you catch other people's gaze and read vague disgust, mockery or simple surprise in their eyes, and it hurts. Think of Lucien de Rubempré in Balzac's *Lost Illusions*: In Blois, he is considered elegant, but when he moves to Paris he suddenly feels as scruffy as a scarecrow. I feel dirty: Look at that white mark on my pullover, the worn sleeves that I had not noticed until now. It is as if I were becoming a tramp before my very own eyes.

After the clothes (which stigmatise you at first glance, before you have even had a chance to say hello), the way you talk, eat and walk will count against you and betray your roots in the lowly world of the toothless, the pitiful and the pathetic – 'the little people, the lowly, the nobodies', in Edmond Rostand's phrase.[1] Your vocabulary, pronunciation and syntax; the way your mouth moves; your clumsy gait and the way you hold your knife like a stake will all betray you.

Childhood is relatively untouched by these formative experiences of shame – they tend to occur in early adolescence. So much fiction and non-fiction has been written about those fateful, shame-filled episodes when you start secondary school. At the age of eleven or twelve, the love of one's family no longer suffices; the family becomes a mere refuge, or else a nightmare. *Who I am* is henceforward a question of *what my status is*, and that is played out in the eyes and words of other people. Who I am is continually being reassessed on the basis of the cards that life deals me. I compare and am compared; I come across others who are richer, stronger, better dressed and more brilliant, and find myself dull and drab in comparison.

This existence in the gaze of others is our hell, our loss of innocence. I am condemned to exist for and through others, a hostage to their judgements, while my own head is bursting with self-assessments and comparisons. Am I on a positive or negative score? What are people going to say about me? 'Classmates' hardly seems like the right word ...

It is at this age that Annie Ernaux *discovers*, in the eyes of others and through their acerbic remarks, that she lives in a rather shabby café-cum-grocery store frequented by drunks. Startled, she forces herself to correct her diction and vocabulary as she learns to identify *the done thing* in this *other* world that is at the same time the real world, by which I mean the one that *counts*. It might constitute a minority numerically, but it sets the axiological benchmark: This is the world to which I want and ought to belong. It is the new object of my desire, and the feeling of being excluded from it drives me mad.

> It's my neighbor who fills me in. You make beds in the morning, oh but yes, every day. 'You must live in a strange house!' The other girls have turned round and are whispering among themselves. Laughter, shouts, and suddenly it turns sour as milk, I see myself, I see myself and I am not like the others ...[2]

Even when they are clean, the poor stink – of bleach. Annie Ernaux recalls one Saturday morning at secondary school just before the essay-writing lesson, when the optician's daughter Jeanne D. exclaimed in disgust: 'It stinks of bleach!' 'I wanted the ground to swallow me up. I hid my hands under the desk, maybe I even put them in the pockets of my blouse. I was out of my mind with shame.'[3] The smell is coming from little Annie, who before leaving for school washed her hands in the kitchen in a basin of water impregnated with the chemical. It is what poor people smell like when they are clean; it is an 'odour of social class'.[4]

Startled, and rather pitifully, we discover that our body language and how we walk, talk and eat is cumbersome and rustic. That there are unknown rites and improbable rules. Anything can provoke the withering disdain of others, and one's own family becomes a well of shame.

> In church, she sang hymns to the Virgin in a loud, booming voice – 'One day I shall meet her in heaven, up in heaven.' It made me want to cry and I hated her for it; I found my own mother's attitude brash. I averted my eyes when she uncorked a bottle, holding it locked between her knees. I was ashamed of her

brusque manners and speech, especially when I realized how alike
we were.[5]

A taste of betrayal in the mouth. Class-based shame reveals a
dimension of society that philosophers (in their abstract reflections
on social pacts, Republican contracts, communities of interest
and the like) and even sociologists regularly overlook. This is
society seen as a hierarchical judgement system, a stigmatising
force and an arena of violent symbolic exclusion and recurring
shame and humiliation. Rich or poor immediately becomes good
or bad, talented or rubbish, beautiful or ugly, top or bottom. I am
either subjected to someone's gaze or fear being subjected to it.
Whether it is openly disdainful, faintly condescending or just a
little surprised and almost amused, this gaze *burns*; so intensely
do I feel the terrible confluence of social, ontological and moral
judgements that it implies and the crushing logic inherent to it:
I do not have much = I am not worth much = I do not amount
to much. I do not have anything = I am not anything. It is a
pyramid whose summit is esteemed and coveted and whose base
is held in contempt. Society is a system for designating allotted
places, and humiliation puts everyone in their place and makes
them aware of their inferior status. The experience of shame is
first and foremost one of being reassigned. I felt alive and unbur-
dened 'at the origin of the world', in Frantz Fanon's phrase, and
now here I am, all of a sudden, relegated to my allotted place.[6] I
discover that worlds exist in the plural, and that they come with
barriers, thresholds and doors. Shame is the painful feeling of a
disjunction, a loss of bearings, a disqualification. Didier Eribon
in *Returning to Reims* notes that talking publicly about his social
background was ultimately more painful than talking about his
homosexuality. 'Let me put it this way: it turned out to be much

easier for me to write about shame linked to sexuality than about shame linked to class.'[7]

The 'class defector' quickly learns how to hide their tracks and hoodwink the new company they keep. You keep tight-lipped to minimise risks; you borrow codes that you've partially gleaned along the way and reproduce them sparingly; you feign indifference, mimic body language and prudently parrot certain turns of phrase. It is a painful, exhausting and petty-minded apprenticeship. At the start of Jack London's eponymous novel, Martin Eden feels his body to be leaden and clumsy – he is the proverbial bull in a china shop. Those first meals and conversations with people who wield their cutlery with elegance and casually toss out literary quotes. How am I supposed to avoid giving myself away at every turn? 'Life is, I think, a blunder and a shame.'[8] Extreme vigilance is required to avoid being found out, to conceal any indication of where you are from. You strive to become invisible, interchangeable (by dint of imitating others) and transparent.

There is also a less common strategy: to wallow in the caricature, exaggerate, lay it on thick and gain acceptance as a buffoon. I play up my social awkwardness and provincialism and make a joke out of it. How terribly funny. At least you have your allotted place, and you control the ridicule and laughter to some extent by inviting it and inventing some of the jokes yourself. You hope for a little tenderness in return, even if it is tinted with scorn. 'That guy makes us laugh.' 'She's a funny one.' Think *The Dinner Game* (*Le Dîner de cons*).[9] You play the fool for others and feel gratitude for being socially accepted. You are inside, nestled in a warm little pocket of scorn, admittedly, but pretty well-positioned. Yes, you are on the lip of that pocket and could fall out at any moment, but *you are still just about within the group.*

๛

Class-based shame is never pure. It contains an ambiguity that is a source of fury – that same fury runs through Annie Ernaux's sentences and invests them with an extreme tension that belies their apparent detachment. Poverty can be unfair, scandalous even beyond a certain threshold, but it is not *necessarily* shameful for all that. It is not the inevitable consequence of being an object of social derision, unlike the objective form of family opprobrium, which demands revenge for a public affront.

To feel the sting of class-based shame, you have to internalise it. To what extent is it *actually* humiliating to live in a café-cum-shop, to have a mother who cleans other people's houses, to own only one pair of trousers that is ironed on Sundays and only one pair of shoes (which happen to be too big for you)? Is a lack of money always, and necessarily, degrading?

A poor person can hold their head up high so long as they do not sink so far into destitution that they have to beg. A woman doing menial work can be proud of the meagre income she scrapes together from the sweat of her brow. And this pride is further bolstered by a nagging suspicion: That guy over there, parading his external signs of wealth? Where did he get his money from? From working? I doubt it somehow. So he is actually the contemptible one.

It is easy enough to see how social disdain can be redirected at the humiliating party, so long as the humiliated party keeps their dignity intact, thereby neutralising the critical gaze that seeks to demean them. All of a sudden, it is the humiliating party who becomes ridiculous and pathetic. Who does he think he is?

There is no need for the cynicism of the Ancient Greeks or the mysticism of the Franciscans (which we will return to) to justify a certain pride in being poor. Those on modest incomes are able to take satisfaction in belonging to a world that could not care less about idiotic social conventions and can make fun of stupid airs and graces and stiff manners. All of that is painful to watch and listen to, and is ultimately demeaning. '*We're* not like that.' None of that fuss. Richard Hoggart wrote some of his finest passages on the us-and-them rhetoric of the working classes and their sense of belonging to a plain-speaking class characterised by communal effort, automatic solidarity, rude health and vigour.[10] This same working-class exuberance explodes from the pages of Gérard Mordillat's *Vive la sociale!*[11]

Ultimately, the real problem with poverty is not so much a lack of wealth as the fear of destitution. It is the rich who are ashamed of not being rich enough. Poor people are haunted by the spectre of destitution, and it is from this perspective that shame hangs over them as the supreme menace. A poor person's dignity is earned the hard way, by warding off penury. Whereas the ethos of the rich is to incite envy, that of the poor is to avoid being a source of shame. It is encapsulated in the line from Annie Ernaux's father, which is detached from the rest of the text, standing out like a painful thorn: 'One day he said to me proudly: "I have never given you cause for shame."'[12] What he no doubt meant by this was that he had never been dishonest ('I owe what I have to my hard work'), never begged ('I avoided destitution'), never shot his mouth off ('I never got above myself'); he had always kept himself clean and presentable. The irony (which would have hurt him, had he known it) being that his clean (but by no means gleaming) café-cum-grocery store *did* make little Annie ashamed.

Beyond all this, there is a dividing line that cuts across class, based not on hierarchies, ranks and quantities (how much do you earn?), but on the boundaries of morality, sex and virtue. My earlier discussion of these may have given the impression that moralising and stigmatising were mainly the preserve of the bourgeois family, but this is by no means the case. Such attitudes have been appropriated and woven into the myth of a virtuous and healthy working class, in contradistinction to a bourgeoisie that is decadent, corrupt and grubby beneath all their finery, as their butlers and maids can attest. People lapped up the first-hand accounts of servants, such as those in Octave Mirbeau's (fictional) *The Diary of a Chambermaid* (1900), with access to the private sphere of the bourgeois family (to their laundry, bed sheets and bodies) who lifted the lid on the hidden baseness behind their employers' hypocritical façade of respectability. It turned out that the bourgeoisie was hiding its moral shame behind all that affectation. One last point worth making is about the pride of the poor. As long as the Marxist view of history (as leading inevitably to the triumph of the proletariat) remained credible, working-class pride could be sustained by an awareness of belonging to a class that was destined for ultimate victory – the class instrument that would save humankind by enabling it to overcome its alienation. Workers could bide their time and savour in advance their coming revenge. The riches of the poor lay in their dreams of the Great Dawn.

To which one might object that this pride of the poor is decidedly twisted – does it not lead directly to social conservatism? We end up in a situation where everyone is satisfied with their social class, and it is the destitution of those at the absolute margins of society that prompts the horror and compassion of all. I think this type of pride is a historical (and dated) phenomenon: a sentimental ethical trope that has been eroded by several decades of neoliberalism. The historical defeat of communism and the end of the grand narratives have contributed to this, but it is, above all, the dogmatic neoliberal insistence on individual responsibility and self-reliance that has transformed poverty into a personal defeat, implying shortcomings of character (such as laziness and a lack of self-discipline and moral fibre) that somehow need addressing. Poverty has become the unequivocal marker of a lack of ambition.

This is perhaps somewhat surprising given that, from the Greek Cynics to Gandhi, the inversion of this class-based shame has been a feature of our culture, often in heroic guises. As is well known, even the most ancient philosophies condemned wealth as false, inauthentic, inessential and immanent (later on, people would call it alienating). But it is one thing not to seek out luxury and to preach austerity and moderation, and quite another to voluntarily deprive oneself of it and to plough a lowly furrow with the same rage and fervour as so many others amass profits. Diogenes the Cynic boasted of having only three possessions: a cloak that served both as a garment and a roof over his head, a pouch containing some bare essentials, and a staff. And yet he would rhapsodise about his situation: My estate is boundless (it has the dimensions of the world); the infinite starry skies are my roof and the lush greenery of nature is where I lay my head. I sleep wherever I happen to stop and I feed on whatever nourishment I may find along the way. If poverty is measured in terms of *how much is lacking*, who could claim to be richer than the Cynic?

> Look at me, I am without a country, without a home, without possessions, without a slave; I sleep out on the ground; I have no wife, no children, no fine residence, but only earth and heaven and one sorry cloak. And what do I lack? Am I not without sorrow, without fear? Am I not free?[13]

One day, Diogenes sees a young boy cupping his hands to drink from the fountain and exclaims: 'A child has beaten me in plainness of living!' He takes his little wooden drinking cup out of his pouch and triumphantly throws it away. It is superfluous to requirements. Possessing *less than before* is not synonymous with becoming poor; on the contrary, it is to lighten one's load. Who could possibly make him feel ashamed of a state of poverty that he boasts of and meticulously refines, all the while voicing his disgust (or alternatively his pity) for the well-off, bulging with all their possessions? Centuries afterwards, Francis of Assisi would take a leaf out of his book, choosing a life of poverty as a challenge to a bloated Church. Later still, Gandhi refused to wear anything but a frayed cotton dhoti; the walking stick that he gripped as he travelled between ashrams was one of his few other worldly possessions.

These singular inverters of social values elevated their poverty into a *cause to be ashamed of wealth*.

The point worth retaining from these radical stances is that social contempt can be sidestepped, deflected and turned back on itself. It only provokes shame if I consent to it at a personal level – by internalising it, I recognise the legitimacy of the system that is condemning me. There are two ways in which this can pan out.

The first involves introjection. In the books of Vincent de Gaulejac and Christophe Dejours, the same conclusion is reached: Shame is the result of the internalising of social contempt.[14] The superior attitude of rich people, with their abrasive arrogance and grimaces of vague disgust, eventually prompts an interior monologue along the lines of: 'It's true that I'm a bit rubbish, it's no surprise that people don't respect me.' Other people's contempt for me turns into self-contempt. I am ashamed in front of my children of belonging to a disparaged class, or of having to put up with the insults of my boss. In this scenario, wise maxims are of scant comfort: They tend to talk only of deliberately chosen and embraced austerity, whereas in most cases poverty is *something endured*, and the dominant social narrative singles out exorbitant revenues as *the* marker of success (as well as the key to freedom and happiness). The boundary condition here can be quiet resignation as shame mellows into calm acceptance: 'He has nothing but contempt for me and he humiliates me, but what am I supposed to do about it? That's just the way things are, and will always be.' A lapse into gentle somnolence that even Victor Hugo's rallying cry in the poem 'To Those Asleep' may struggle to disturb: 'Awaken and cast your shame aside!'[15]

The second scenario is that of raging ambition. The contempt of others scalds me and I cannot handle it. It spawns bitterness: 'Just you wait.' I feel a quiet fury at being disparaged and made to feel inferior, when I consider myself to be every bit their equal. 'Who does he think he is? Come to that, who does he take me for? One of these days, he'll get his comeuppance.' All these toxic hierarchies are seemingly contingent and unfair (birth, inheritance). And so a plan for revenge takes shape in seething isolation. Through sheer hard work (or cynical calculation), I will soon be the one they respect, the person they desperately want to claim they know. My ambition is boundless but must be concealed (I have to rein in my sarcasm).

This ambition not only actively feeds off class-based shame but is somewhat paradoxical if one thinks these rather unhealthy day-dreams through to their logical conclusion: 'Just you wait, when I make it, it will be my turn to dismiss your eager solicitations, to act as if you were invisible, and to find you pathetic.' Daydreams of glorious future revenge. In this scenario, ambition acts to endorse a system that may belittle me now but one day will laud me – it is simply a matter of time. *I too* fully intend to join the patronising

classes. *I will show them what I am made of.* Does my burning desire
to be one of them mean that I ultimately identify more with the
humiliators than the humiliated? The boundary condition here
is anger. Raging ambition is driven by self-interest, but anger
contains within it a demand for justice (anger in some sense burns
off the unhealthy emotions associated with ambition). This has a
positive effect in that the reaction to being scorned is not limited
to introjection ('They're right, I'm useless') or personal ambition
('I'll show them they're wrong about me'). In *Rhetoric*, Aristotle
identifies anger as the correct response to a slight (*oligôria*: treating
somebody as of little account), expressing, as it does, the determination to restore one's self-respect after it has been undermined
by the disdain of others.[16] This should not be misunderstood as
a variation on the theme of clan vengeance (settling a score on
a point of lost honour through an act of revenge); rather, I am
suggesting that vengeance of a political or aesthetic nature can be
a more dignified means of overcoming shame than mere vengeful
ambition. It is what Annie Ernaux called 'avenging my race'.[17]
We will return to this question in more depth shortly.

A defining characteristic of political shame is that it is self-
reflexive. A line from Camus in *The First Man* will serve to clarify
what I mean by this. Little Jacques (the author's literary double)
begins secondary school, having won a scholarship to go there
thanks to his primary school teacher. He is asked in class to specify
his parents' profession on his introduction form. His father is dead
and his mother cleans other people's houses to feed the family.
He hesitates: Should I put 'housewife'? No, whispers one of his
classmates. You should put 'servant' because 'housewife' means
something else. But surely 'servant' means a skivvy or a slave?
And all of a sudden, he's ashamed because his mother does indeed
work as a domestic servant for others.

Camus is quick to convey the painful, double-edged nature of the child's shame: If I am ashamed of my mother, it must be because I find her contemptible, whereas what she is in fact doing is wearing herself down to the bone to put food on the table for us. So, suddenly, I am ashamed of being ashamed. 'Jacques started to write the word, stopped, and all at once he knew shame and all at once the shame of having been ashamed.'[18]

The two do not belong to the same register. The first internalises the contempt. The second is a shudder of realisation – a feeling of indignation and anger at oneself for having been so prompt to betray and implicitly endorse an iniquitous system of values. What little Jacques confusedly realises is that, even if his mother is a servant, she is not working for *other people*: She is working for her *children*.

4

A Ghost Story

The basic distinction we have drawn so far between public shame (brought about by the opinion of others) and private guilt (welling up from my inner being) is somewhat rough and ready. Things are actually a good deal more complex. It is always *towards another person* (whom I might have unfairly offended or cruelly neglected and whose pain haunts me) that I feel guilty. Whereas shame could be encapsulated in the refrain 'me, me, me'. In realising that I am a hostage to the opinion of others, I become aware too that I am a slave to my own image.

Nothing is ultimately more intimate than shame, but it is an intimate space whose waters are muddied by the tread of others. To understand shame, one has to give up the neat distinction between 'me' and 'others'. Montaigne observed that there is 'as much difference between us and ourselves as there is between us and others', and one is frankly tempted to go further and assert that there is *more* distance between us and ourselves than us and others.[1]

At a certain level of analysis, the distinction between *me* and *others* breaks down. Mentally, the two wholes disintegrate and spill over into each other. The self is formed of others but, even then, it is not a compact whole but rather an array of fragments (parents, friends, colleagues) amid which one catches the glint of various facets of the self. The clearly demarcated boundaries of my body might suggest that it has a single and stable owner, but that is merely a 'useful fiction', to borrow Nietzsche's phrase. Far from being a compact nucleus or a discrete identity, the self is encumbered with ghosts and is torn and divided. The distinct entity that is my body is only a unit at the macrobiological level. In recent decades, immunology has taught us that life is a continuous series of transactions involving colonies of micro-organisms and hosting arrangements that are forever being renegotiated with bacteria, viruses and parasites. And the mental self is just as pluralistic, patched together and peopled by the ghosts of others (unless it is the other way around, and it is the real traces of others that weave together the ghost of a self). In order to get to grips with this complex dance, I propose borrowing three concepts from psychoanalysis. From its founding premises (the unconscious, repression, and so on) emerged a picture of consciousness as a fragmented archipelago – as froth on the surface being tossed around by deeper currents. A series of dancing figures parade through the psyche, at once reflections of the self and purveyors of the demands of others, Of these, I have identified three that give rise to distinct types of shame: the *superego*, the *ideal ego* and the *ego ideal*.

The first question is, can we be ashamed in front of ourselves, and if so, to what extent? The experiences of shame that make for the best stories are those involving the scathing gaze of the other; the mental suffering caused by their contempt, disdain and mockery; and the feeling of emptiness, the embarrassment at even existing, the desperate desire for the ground to swallow us up. Shame always seems to be connected to the appearance and agency of another person. Nudity, dirtiness and vice are only shameful in front of another person, as Sartre famously explored in his play *No Exit*.[2]

And, yet, if others make themselves at home *within me* in the guise of floating phantoms, and if many of my personal characteristics are in fact the traces or imprints left by others, then what we call solitude is a very relative concept. I am never as alone as all that, and others are not necessarily external to me. When someone commits atrocities with impunity, gives into the temptation of corruption, or otherwise behaves in an abject manner, people will typically remark: 'Has he no shame? How can he look himself in the mirror?' Here it is clearly a question of being ashamed in relation to oneself, but we are not really talking about the conscious self that is aware of itself and the world around it (the cognitive entity with a faculty for integrating experiences studied by psychologists). We are talking about our moral conscience, which resembles an inner eye – that same unanswerable and implacable eye that 'was looking at Cain' in the Victor Hugo poem.[3]

This lofty moral eye looking down on us even in our private moments is conceived of as the presence of the supreme Other within us. 'God thinking', in Hugo's words.[4] It is an eye that is simultaneously within and without. Kant, in a text on the 'internal court', assimilates it to a judge by whom everyone is 'observed, threatened, and, in general, kept in awe (respect coupled with fear)'.[5] A judge who follows you like a shadow that you cannot escape, with a voice that you cannot block out. But, for my own conscience to be my judge, and for me to fear it, some sort of internal division has to take place whereby I perceive it as slightly dissociated from me – as a transcendent entity looking down on me. In a sense, I stand in judgement before myself, but this second me is another. Freud subsequently forges the concept of the *superego*, which replaces Kantian abstractions (conscience as a higher judge, the idea of humanity subsisting within me) with more concrete figures: My conscience is the product of introjected parental censure – the internalising of the strict, castrating father. Alternatively, one might prefer to this family-orientated scenario a sociological perspective that sees conscience as the repository of social rules, but the essential structure remains the same. Conscience is always described as that part of me which is the representative or imprint within me of the Other (God, Judge, Father, Society, and so on), before which I am perfectly capable of feeling ashamed because it is felt to be a distinct, disassociated authority. At this point, the distinction between shame and guilt becomes more porous, but the horror is still there, in any case, as is the suffering caused by exposure to this all-seeing eye. This is moral shame.

The second Freudian spectre is the *ideal ego*, which gives rise to a different manifestation: narcissistic shame. The ideal ego refers to that part of ourselves that emerges from the fantasy of omnipotence and complete mastery of the environment. It is the tyrannical self that finds fulfilment in overstating its own merits, basks in imagined power scenarios and brooks no constraints. In this context, shame takes the form of a downfall, a crashing into the rocks of reality: It is the moment when the pretentious person is unmasked or the overconfident child experiences failure and ridicule. It is the sorry defeat of somebody with a high opinion of themselves who hits the buffers of reality, which will always shatter their illusions of omnipotence. Narcissistic shame relates to this moment of defeat when the scales fall from their eyes.

For many a psychoanalyst, it is a firm favourite. It affords them an opportunity to moralise, encouraging the abandonment of impossible desires and establishing the acceptance of harsh realities as the benchmark of a successful course of therapy. Shame becomes a marker of a virtuous transition from psychosis to neurosis, from the obliging imaginary to the challenging symbolic.[6] It is the emotional indicator of the monstrosity of desire, the sage acceptance of the finite and part of the process of learning from one's disappointments.

It is by no means my intention here to downplay the importance of narcissistic shame, but I do want to take issue with the shaming that this model can sometimes be used to justify, with the analyst becoming the secular giver of lessons on impossible desires and the self-appointed representative on earth of the reality principle. As a matter of fact, our existences are replete with these painful reminders of the need for humility, patience and exacting standards. Indeed, patterns of behaviour designed to systematically avoid such knockbacks, driven by the terror of falling victim to them, could even be deemed pathological. Major signs of such shame aversion include narcissistic rage and narcissistic perversion. The narcissistic pervert devotes himself to shaming the other (a female partner, friend or lover) through constant reminders of this type in order to block and prevent any outbreak of shame within himself – making the partner or friend ashamed as she becomes aware of her uselessness, for example.[7] Narcissistic rage, meanwhile, might be described as a form of furious rejection of any challenge to one's ego – an enraged reaction to a situation that threatens to make one feel inferior.[8] An uncontrollable fit of anger laden with insults and recriminations against a world that is profoundly unfair. Rather than learning from one's failures, one casts oneself as a total victim and takes the sting out of the narcissistic wounds by working oneself up into a wild fury.

I foresee a potential objection here: In the case of narcissistic shame, is it not difficult to make room inside for the ghost of the other? Is not the other squeezed out by the excessive affirmation of the self? Freud himself indicates the answer when he ironically refers to 'His Majesty the Baby' in his introductory essay on narcissism.[9] At first sight, this might seem to refer to the way in which the infant embodies the pleasure principle: It is the age of primary narcissism. But in using the term *His Majesty*, Freud is driving at something else: This delirious self-love has been nurtured and shaped by parental love – maternal devotion, paternal worship – to such a degree that the self is only ever a crucible of identifications (in this case, the parents projecting themselves onto the child). Everybody knows, moreover, that the narcissist requires an audience: Self-adoration thrives best in front of a crowd of swooning onlookers.

And finally, there is a third type of shame that we will dub *social-ideal* that corresponds to Freud's concept of the *ego ideal*. The ego in question here corresponds to how we would fervently like to be seen and spoken of by others. It involves the social role models that I endeavour to imitate – figures who are sometimes so exemplary, admired and revered that the disparity between me and them is crushing. I do not *identify* with these splendid individuals in dubious narcissistic orgies. Instead, they float all around me and inspire self-loathing. I am 'not enough' like this, 'too much' like that, simply 'not as I should be'. I am constantly ashamed, but it is not the sporadic wounds inflicted by external reality that are the cause. Rather, I make myself feel ashamed through continually comparing myself unfavourably to others – an ambivalent soliloquy that merely serves to make me disappointed with myself. But should we view this as an acid that gradually corrodes my self-confidence or a healthy form of humility that enables me to move forward? An endless and inevitably doomed quest for recognition or a positive shaping of my character in relation to demanding role models?

The book by Betty Friedan that so unsettled the America of the early 1960s focused its criticism on this self-deprecating impulse against a backdrop of alienating ideals. She showed how the much-vaunted wonders of the American way of life – consumer society, material comfort, the freedom that new household appliances and means of communication were supposed to give housewives so that they could devote themselves fully to their children, their own bodies, their beauty, their husband and his career – were saccharine stereotypes of happiness and a fulfilled family life. Relentlessly promoted by advertising, their principal and extremely widespread effect was to make women ashamed – these were ubiquitously oppressive ideals. They inevitably felt like bad mothers, bad wives and failed women when they acknowledged to themselves that living in a nice suburban house with a garden and looking after the family did not in fact make them especially happy, that there were perhaps limits to the pleasure to be had in telling off the children, sleeping with their husband and making dinner. Happiness (or rather the image thereof) can be depressing if it involves the enactment of an ideal. The image of happiness shames the woman who is depressed on account of her dissatisfaction. Her frustration condemns her to chasing after commodities that are supposed to procure or embody happiness, but which in fact are designed to disappoint her.[10]

Once again, the ego ideal turns out to be the ideal of other people: either the ambitions of family members that I would like to realise in order to please them, or else social conventions underpinned by big business. Ultimately, we are talking parental projections or stereotyped desires. At times, my shame is less a case of not living up to my own standards than failing to meet the expectations of others. The shame of the daughter who does not succeed in life as her parents would have wished, the shame of not being the nice, cool guy who is popular among his peers. I prove myself unworthy by not obtaining the qualifications or salary expected of somebody of my social class. With a job that is not highly regarded socially, I fear that my friends and even my own children will think I am 'not up to it'.

There is one final conceptual turn of the screw. We have seen how what are taken to be ideals of the self (of the ego ideal) are, in fact, the ideals of others. But that is without reckoning on this: What my parents or friends would like to see me be is above all what I imagine they'd like me to be. We're suddenly a long way from the mere automatic introjection of external ideals: Shame is the expression of a desperate, naked desire to be liked, quite simply.

These three types of shame all involve feeling inferior and denigrated in relation, respectively, to a despotic morality, an implacable reality or a tyrannical ideal. When you think about it, we spend an awful lot of our lives striving to make a good impression, making sacrifices for ghosts and forcing ourselves to correspond to what we believe to be other people's expectations. An awful lot of time, in other words, desperately trying, with every fibre in our bodies, to exorcise or ward off these three forms of shame. Our absolute imperative is to dupe the world, even if it means lying furiously to ourselves.

The Romand affair in France can be seen as a tragedy born out of a terrible fear of shame.[11] The basic facts of the case are as follows. On the morning of 9 January 1993, Jean-Claude Romand murdered his wife and two children. He then drove over to his parents' house and killed them in cold blood too, along with their dog. That same evening, he travelled to Fontainebleau with the intention of killing his mistress as well. He spent the next day at home alone in the presence of the three corpses. In the early hours of the morning, he swallowed some barbiturates and then set fire to his house, making sure the windows were wide open, but the fire brigade was alerted soon enough to save him from the flames. As soon as he awoke from a brief coma, investigators began to question him, and their suspicions were soon aroused.

In due course, the investigating magistrate and psychiatrists patiently reconstructed a virtually unthinkable chain of events. Romand confessed not only to the five murders but to a lifetime of lies and deceit – for twenty long years, he had lied to everyone, from his wife and parents to his friends and neighbours. He had deceived and abused the trust of everyone in his entourage, and absolutely no one had been in on the secret. He claimed to be a medical researcher at the World Health Organization and, every morning, put on a suit and kissed his wife and children goodbye before supposedly heading off to work. But, in reality, he spent his days cooped up in his car in motorway service stations reading medical journals. Sometimes he would go for a little walk in the surrounding woods. And nobody suspected a thing.

Back in September 1975, he had celebrated passing his end-of-year medical exam with his parents. He smiled modestly when they congratulated him, but little did they know that he had not even shown up for the exam. In the years that followed, he kept registering again for his second year of medical studies so that he could keep his student card, attend the faculty and frequent the libraries. He would talk about his new classes and celebrate passing each successive exam. His life became a fabric of falsehoods – a spiral of lies that soon became impossible for him to own up to. At a certain point, he crossed a threshold and was simply unable to rip off the mask that he had donned when he first announced to his delighted parents that he had passed his exam – the mask had become his face. A tragedy born out of a fear of shame. To carry off this deception over a period of twenty years and afford his family a standard of living commensurate with his supposed professional status, he ripped off his parents, parents-in-law and friends, promising them huge returns on investment if they entrusted him with their savings and occasional windfalls (such as a property sale), so long as they were patient and discreet. And they were only too willing to do so, imagining no doubt that they were on to a good thing with a WHO doctor working in Geneva.

The psychiatric experts tasked with assessing the impostor went down the 'ideal ego' route, diagnosing a pathology of a narcissistic nature. Their report highlights his traumatic experiences at the prestigious Lycée du Parc in Lyon, where, in 1971, he embarked on a crammer course. But, as well as being subjected to a humiliating initiation ritual, he suddenly found himself – the son of a forest warden – in the company of sons of doctors, lawyers and academics, and some highly intelligent people ('I was entering the temple of the intellect'). It was more than he could bear: In early November, he fell ill and jacked it all in. A few years later in June, he overslept for his end-of-year medical exam. Then, for the September exams, he had a bad fall just beforehand that should have prevented him from taking them, but his parents insisted on driving him to the centre themselves. He never crossed the threshold of the hall, but, in the evening, he told them everything had gone well.

Emmanuel Carrère's book about this case, *The Adversary*, leans more towards the 'ego ideal' theory. At the price of lying, Jean-Claude doggedly embraced a socially respected profession to the point of losing his own identity: 'behind his social façade he was nothing'; 'shedding the skin of Dr Romand would mean ending up without any skin, more than naked: flayed'.[12] Living in shame is, above all, a case of living in terror of having to endure it.

Romand was released in June 2019 and, having found God in prison, lived in seclusion in a monastery until leaving in 2022. He is now completely free. By exposing his shame to the eternal gaze of God – by making it a matter of the superego – he completes the hat trick of Freudian spectres.

These three ghosts of the Other within me (superego, ideal ego and ego ideal) should not be regarded as separate impermeable entities. Freud himself never clearly distinguished between the latter two, being well aware that excessive (or deficient) self-love and being loved too much (or too little) by others tend to overlap and reinforce each other. The tyrannical superego, meanwhile, plays the game of ego ideal by setting ever more exacting standards and indulges the ideal ego by encouraging masochistic pleasures. Each entity seeks out the complicity of the others.

Indeed, one might be justified in asserting that, in the present age, these three types of shame (moral, narcissistic and social ideal) are systematically superimposed, merging in a dizzying spiral rather than operating in a dialectical manner. In the age of dominant theories (when society was neurotic, or convention-bound, or guilt-ridden), these entities were tethered to stable points (the law structured the superego, norms shaped the ego ideal and sin contained the ideal ego) such that they formed three corners of a triangle: indissociable but separate. But, in recent decades, the existence in every domain (whether personal, professional or family) of an ideal of performance has triggered a dynamic that whizzes them all up together: There is a tyrannical injunction (superego) to love oneself (ideal ego) courtesy of the social recognition that goes with a well-regarded and fulfilling job (ego ideal). So-called neoliberalism, in its ethical dimension, is the creation of this spiral: *Fulfil yourself to the max in your amazing job – that's an order!* The alternative is shame.

Kafka wrote the final chapter of *The Trial* before all the others, as early as 1914. In reading the final sentence (the one that really cut through with Primo Levi) – '"Like a dog!" he said; it was as if the shame of it must outlive him,' I wonder why so many critics have declared *The Trial* to be the quintessential novel about shame.[13] Although the sense of strangeness in reading it does indeed come in part from the flitting, ghostly harbingers of guilt (unlikely judges, unlocatable courtrooms, bizarre law clerks) that surround him, Joseph K. himself never behaves like a guilty man. Deep down, he does not feel guilty, just a bit overwhelmed by events. He feels by turns surprised, irritated and ultimately rather worried by the way things seem to be panning out.

When his two nemeses come to his place to arrest him at the end of the book, he does not put up any resistance. But it is not so much a case of deferring to an unconscious guilt – his reaction is a mix of incredulity, defeatism and a desire not to make a scene. His executioners eventually find a piece of wasteland to serve as his place of execution, at which point K. notices in the distance an individual gesticulating from the top-floor window of a house on the edge of the quarry. One of the executioners 'thrust the knife deep into his heart and turned it there twice'.[14]

He dies 'like a dog', as if he is not even capable of dying properly. Slaughtered like a common animal with somebody looking on. What I should have done, when there was still time, was grab the knife and heroically plunge it into my stomach, but now it's too late. That would have been a more decent end than pathetically allowing myself to be put to death like that. That said, things got off to a bad start: The 'partners' dispatched to execute me were absurdly clumsy.

Similar is the woman committing suicide who, before losing consciousness altogether, belatedly notices a grease stain on her shirt. The man standing in front of the firing squad who realises, just before the rifles go off, that his laces are undone. 'Oh no, that too?'

That is the faint background music that ultimately accompanies us throughout our lives, right to the very end. Not the crashing organ chords of sin and guilt, but the persistent chatter of shame. This is the cruel irony of Kafka's story. K.'s final minute on earth is not a moment of profound reflection or piercing insight. Instead, he is concerned about a blot on his reputation: My death is distinctly lacking in class. And the worst of it, writes Primo Levi, is that 'that's more or less how all of us will die'.[15]

We will devote our last instants on earth to wondering: 'Am I up to it, am I coming across as likeable enough?'

> If I closely examine what is my ultimate aim, it turns out that I am not really striving to be good and to fulfil the demands of a Supreme Judgement, but rather very much the contrary: I strive to know the whole human and animal community, to recognize their basic predilections, desires, moral ideals, to reduce these to simple rules and as quickly as possible trim my behaviour to these rules in order that I may find favour in the whole world's eyes.[16]

The final sentence of the novel is 'as if the shame of it must outlive him'. Kafka writes 'as if' because he knows perfectly well that the rest of the world could not give a damn and that shame never survives. An entire existence, right up to the last second, dominated by a fear of ridicule and pathetic strategies to win the favour of other people who actually could not care less, so preoccupied are they by their own efforts to come across well.

But that is how it is: We spend an entire lifetime asking ourselves how we should live, talk, love and die. We are forever striving to make the grade, but in relation to what and to whom? Nobody has the faintest idea.

5

Melancholy

So far, we have looked at two states of mind that can generate shame: disdain (which has to do with hierarchies) and indignation (which has to do with virtue). There also exists a third: insurmountable disgust. This is the shame of being seen as – or feeling oneself to be – pitiful, revolting and dirty. Discrimination can be of a social, moral or physical nature, and the power of the final scene of *L'Assommoir* derives from the superimposition of all three registers in Zola's depiction of the demise of Gervaise.[1] Destitute, filthy and obese, she tries pathetically to sell her 'charms' in the street but is suddenly overwhelmed with shame when she sees her own huge, hideous shadow cast by the streetlamp.

The shame associated with filth has fascinated psychoanalysts specialising in the pre-Oedipal phases, who see it as capturing the ambiguity of toilet training: initial encouragement ('Well done!') that is soon contradicted by disgusted discouragement ('Yuck!'). In his preface to an American dissertation on scatological rites, Freud went further and asserted that men and women, in being ashamed of their excrement, are expressing the sheer embarrassment prompted by this 'remnant of Earth'.[2] There is no cleansing ourselves of our own body (of its needs, discharges, heaviness and thickness), and being ashamed of dirt is ultimately about being ashamed of the body itself, a persistent and deflating reminder of our earthly nature: We are not pure spirits, and our ideals of purity and dreams of being diaphanous collapse on the physical mass of our body. This is the radical, existential shame of Ellen West as described by the Swiss psychiatrist Ludwig Binswanger.[3] In the same vein, Max Scheler writes that modesty is 'the mind blushing at the body'.[4] The body is decidedly a source of shame for the soul.

Still in the same vein, there is the oppressive cultural cliché that assimilates menstruation to an impure stain – something that has to be hidden and must not be spoken of.[5] It was not so long ago that girls learnt of the existence of periods when, much to their astonishment and distress, they had their first one – only then did their mothers take them aside and quietly explain what was going on. It is as if there was necessarily shame attached to becoming aware of oneself as a woman; as if, from the very outset, there was something taboo about one's new status as a fertile, sexual being. Even before one considers women's often inferior social status – which, one might argue, is historically determined, contingent and correctable, even if it is recurrent – the shame of being a woman appears to be a staple of culture and people's mindsets. Psychoanalysis has hardly helped matters with its tendency to cleave to Freudian orthodoxy and the dubious notion that female desire is shaped and haunted by penis envy – that girls and women are to be defined by a lack. By employing a vocabulary of deficiency, deficit and absence, psychoanalysis has implicitly but de facto turned female sexuality into a burden of shame.

❧

These three principal domains of shame (social inferiority, moral infamy and physical uncleanliness) entail scathing insults and crippling humiliations. More precisely, when somebody else suddenly looks at me, categorises me and judges me, I feel that I have been relegated, rejected and excluded from the community of 'decent', 'normal', 'respectable' and 'likeable' people (or sometimes from the human race full stop), at which point, I start to lose my grip. In a slight panic I realise that everyday civilities (standard formulas of politeness or even neutral indifference) had until now served to anchor me, not that I had been aware of it. Now that I am overcome with shame, the feeling is akin to losing one's grip and falling. In their embarrassment, the shy person folds their arms and hangs their head. They can feel the ground collapsing under their feet and are trying hard not to fall. They had been clinging to the group and believed they were a branch of the social tree, and, all of a sudden, it is as though they no longer have anything to hold on to. We could turn this around and assert that physical disgust, moral disdain and social indignation are all ways of unifying the group, which becomes of its own accord the repository of the majority view.

Political philosophers have tended to converge on a common answer to the question of how a society comes to be, which is to say how you transition from a 'multitude' (an anarchic juxtaposition of individuals) to a 'people' (a coherent community). Indulging in thought experiments, they have come up with the idea of a 'social contract' or foundational pact wherein an assembly of rational actors unanimously agrees to exercise self-restraint and delegate responsibility for laying down common rules to a sole authority. This is a rational genealogy of society, and yet it is well known that passions unify and reason divides. This myth of the rational pact holds sway in the realm of books and lectures, but the only thing it reconciles is the thinker with their thoughts.

It is actually passions such as fear, hate and sectarian worship that delineate and hive off a distinct community. Each defines a specific domain that is external to it: the *outside* (hostile passions), the *transcendent* (idol-worshipping passions) or the *margin* (shameful passions).

Hostile communities are straightforward to define. It is easy enough to see that there is nothing like hatred and fear to knit together a collective. It is by offering up an enemy to hate or an outsider to fear that a people coalesces and a group is bound together. The enemy makes us forget internal divisions and ancient quarrels, generating a shared identity – an 'Us' with a capital *U* – that must be preserved against any contamination. All the usual frustrations, corrosive jealousies and bitter resentments that normally bedevil communal living magically fade away before the threatening spectre of the outside, prompting the community to pull together. It is the logic of the scapegoat.

Idol-worshipping communities overcome jealous rivalries and entrenched competing interests by projecting a golden image of a transcendent supreme being. Among siblings, the nagging question is: Is someone else my parent's favourite? It can poison one's existence and is the prototype of all resentments. By contrast, a supreme being (so infinitely superior to us that he cannot prefer anyone) renders everyone equal when worshipping him. La Boétie saw in this spell cast over us the secret of politically structured societies: 'fascinated and so to speak bewitched by the name of one man alone'.[6] The fetishising of a single supreme being makes us forget our differences and brings us together in shared veneration.

And, lastly, there are shame-based communities. In this case, the group forms around its shared revulsion for an individual who

is portrayed as vice incarnate. After the outside and the transcendent, we have the margin. The image of Hester Prynne in the first
chapter of *The Scarlet Letter* (1850) comes to mind. She is exposed
to public opprobrium outside the gates of a Boston prison for
having committed adultery. She has in her arms her little girl –
whose father she refuses to name – and a red *A* has been woven
into her dress like a blood stain. The whole community, gathered
around her, shudders in disgust. I recall as well the photographs of
the shaven-headed women after the liberation of France in 1945:
mocking faces and evil stares, and the women themselves looking
blank or lost or distressed – in particular, there is the woman in
Le Havre holding her infant tightly to her breast in the midst of
the jeering crowd.[7] I think too of the school kid being made fun
of in the playground. Gaggles of children stamping their feet in
mirth as tears well up in the eyes of the girl everyone is pointing
at or of the little boy being bullied. And the cruel pleasure felt
by all the others in being out of the firing line – the secret relief
that I am not in the other's shoes, because I am acutely aware of
how similar we are. And I join in with the chorus of jeering to
suppress the feelings that this spectacle of distress awakens in me.

At the heart of the terrible pain of being singled out and made
to feel inferior is a desperate sense of having been abandoned,
which is a source of much of the anguish. The Hungarian psychoanalyst Imre Hermann had an outlandish idea that he attempted
to back up scientifically in his writings.[8] How did it occur to him?
Perhaps by observing infants' first gestures – the way their tiny
hands reach out and grip onto things. Perhaps in looking at prints
of young monkey mothers calmly going about their business with
their little ones clinging to their stomachs or backs. The hairier
the better, from the point of view of forming bonds. Hermann
posited a *primary clinging instinct* as a kind of physical referent

of the 'need for attachment' later theorised by John Bowlby, and speculated that our species' relative hairlessness, which is not at all conducive to clinging, is the source of an unspoken but persistent anxiety within us that is the cause of all our distress (anxiety, guilt, shame).[9] On this view, the distress associated with shame derives from a feeling of abandonment – a sense of the group letting go of us, of finding ourselves in the void, detached from the whole, our bonds severed.

Maupassant's *Boule de Suif* tells the tale of a group of travellers fleeing occupied Rouen in a stagecoach. There are three couples (vulgar social climbers, bourgeois opportunists and self-satisfied aristocrats), two nuns, a democrat and finally a plump prostitute (Boule de Suif), who is initially given the cold shoulder by these members of 'respectable' society, who are indignant at having to share the confined carriage space with a harlot (though the democrat Cornudet is somewhat amused by the situation). The story unfolds against the routing of the French army by the Prussians in 1870, which was a source of great patriotic shame for an entire nation. Thick snow hampers the stagecoach's progress, time drags, and it becomes clear that they will not be reaching a hostel any time soon. But the pretty brunette who makes a living from her ample charms saves the day: To avoid spending too much at inns, she has prepared a picnic basket full of food. She starts wolfing it down while everybody else's stomach rumbles, but then she offers to share her feast out of natural bonhomie. The hungry stomachs of all these respectable people win out over their moral reservations, and they willingly and greedily accept her offer.

Second act. They reach the inn, which is occupied by Prussian forces, and get a good night's sleep, but, the next day, the stagecoach cannot leave because an officer has forbidden the coachman to saddle the horses. The previous night, the staunch patriot Boule de Suif turned down the officer's request for a 'night of passion', and he has no intention of allowing them to leave unless she changes her mind and complies with his request. The travellers are naturally outraged by this despicable demand and intolerable blackmail. But the days pass by, seemingly ever more slowly, and boredom sets in, then irritation and finally anger at being detained in this place. And it is not so much the libidinous Prussian officer whom they blame as the strumpet, who is being inordinately patriotic. Is it not her profession, after all? Each one of them attempts to persuade her that placating the officer is in the common interest. The nuns go a step further, telling the devoutly religious Boule de Suif that it would be a great act of martyrdom. This finally convinces her, and she gives in.

Third act. Everyone crowds around the coach, which is now ready to depart, but studiously avoids Boule de Suif's gaze – she has been ostracised once again. They seem to be embarrassed, but about what? About what she agreed to endure, or the fact that each of them in their own way had pressured her to give in? Whatever the case, she receives not a word of thanks or comfort. Over the course of several hours in the carriage, no one speaks to her or even looks at her. The time comes to eat, but this time Boule de Suif has not stocked up on supplies. The virtuous nuns and respectable couples noisily tuck into their own provisions but offer nothing to the woman whose sacrifice enabled them to depart and whose picnic basket is now as empty as their consciences. Cornudet whistles 'La Marseillaise' and Boule de Suif sobs quietly as everyone chomps away.

Flaubert considered this story to be a true masterpiece, and it is not just the dramatic structure that is impressive. There is a cruel lucidity in Maupassant: Giving violent expression to our own monstrous proclivities is part and parcel of moral outrage. What we are expunging is our own dark side. The social respectability of the cowardly is bought at the price of excluding others. 'Shame on you!' goes the cry, as if one could thereby expel that which lies deeply buried within oneself. Mingled with the tears of Boule de Suif is bitterness and plenty of anger, directed both at the others and herself. She has been reassigned to her allotted place: For all your generosity and selflessness, you'll only ever be a whore. She is angry at herself for having been so naive as to think that the social barriers could come tumbling down, ashamed for having believed it, and now bitterly conscious that she has been jettisoned.

Some psychologists have wondered whether it is possible for infants to feel shame – an unlikely question that would appear impossible to answer. They have sought to get around the obvious difficulties by searching for apparent signs, such as a lowering of the head, the dangling of their arms, or an empty look in the eyes. And they believe they have spotted a tell-tale sign at the moment when the mother removes her breast without warning from the baby's mouth.[10] Sometimes, instead of crying insistently for more, they will react with a kind of defeatism, a sad resignation, which one might be tempted to interpret as a template for, or at least a gestural intimation of, the melancholic shame that they will later feel: the shame of having believed it for a moment, of having imagined that they could be loved, admired and appreciated just a little. It is the shame of abandonment, which, in this instance, is engendered not by the gaze of the other but, on the contrary, by the indifference with which that gaze turns away.

The fear, indeed the unshakeable certainty, of not being loved forming in the pit of my stomach this frozen lake, which is placid yet can feel like a lead weight. But so what? Life goes on, even if I do feel a little ashamed.

6

The Total Social Fact: Incest and Rape (Traumatic Shame)

The experiences of shame that we *endure* are traumatic in that they leave traces. Memory, writes Annie Ernaux, is shame's special gift: 'I am endowed by shame's vast memory, more detailed and implacable than any other, a gift unique to shame.'[1] We recall humiliating scenes with great precision – they carve clear, sharply delineated shapes within us. Though it is possible that it works the other way round and the trauma actually gives rise to a specific shame: Suffering arises from the obscure but fatalistic conviction that the event somehow singled me out. I am ashamed because *this is happening specifically to me*.

Robert Antelme reports an episode where the SS, with the Allies bearing down on them, abandon the concentration camps, taking along the horde of prisoners and randomly shooting one from time to time to keep the rest moving. At one point, an Italian is abruptly singled out – 'Come here you!' – and rather than going white, the young man goes red. It seems scarcely imaginable that his reaction to being picked out from the crowd should be to blush with shame, given that the object is to kill him. What tenacious mechanism must lurk within us for an unexpected 'You there!' to elicit a shame that outweighs the terror of dying?

'*Du, komme her!*' Another Italian steps out of the column, a student from Bologna. I know him. I look at him. His face has turned pink. I look at him closely. I still have that pink before my eyes. He stands there at the side of the road. He doesn't know what to do with his hands either. He seems embarrassed ... He turned pink after the SS man said to him, '*Du, komme her!*' He must have glanced about him before he flushed; but yes, it was he who had been picked, and when he doubted it no longer, he turned pink. The SS who was looking for a man, any man, to kill had found him.'[2]

The trauma is the event that instils in me the shame of having been chosen, of having been 'found'.

At the end of the nineteenth century, Jean-Martin Charcot proposed the first medical definition of this, selecting as his examples sudden and brutal accidents (explosions, collisions, derailments, and so on) which, although they did not occasion any detectable anatomic lesions, left the affected individuals with persistent and debilitating symptoms, such as spasms, paralysis, a withdrawal into silence, headaches and shaking. By way of explanation, Charcot posited the prior existence within these traumatised subjects of a 'hysterical' inclination in the sense of fragile nerves. On this view, the traumatic dimension is not due to the objective gravity of the triggering event but the subject's congenital vulnerability, which in a sense is revealed or activated by the shock. This diagnosis cast a long cultural shadow of shame, particularly over those traumatised by war. There was the sexist shame of being reduced to a nervous little girl by the medical profession: If you were traumatised, it was because you had a weak constitution and feeble nerves. The tragedy of the shell-shocked soldiers of the First World War lies in the fact that the victims were treated at best as having weak temperaments, fragile nerves and feminine sensibilities, and at worst as impostors and malingerers. Either way, they would be known as the 'soldiers of shame'.[3]

The shift in the meaning of trauma in the second half of the twentieth century is attributable to immense historical and personal tragedies, ranging from those endured by Holocaust survivors to those experienced by Vietnam veterans, victims of terrorist attacks and children born of incestuous relationships.[4] The treatment of such patients, in particular through a diagnosis of post-traumatic stress disorder (DSM-III), has become ever more sympathetic, and we have done away with Charcot's oppressive and disparaging theoretical edifice. Contrary to what he asserted, it is indeed the events in themselves that are traumatic through their sheer scale and the objective harm they do, and there is no shame in being profoundly affected by such horrors. And yet, in the case of sexual assaults (rape, incest and other sexual abuse), a kernel of specific and irreducible shame resurfaces.[5]

By way of illustration, here are three cases of women whose experiences and sheer resoluteness altered the history of rape and incest.

Firstly, there is the case of biology teacher Anne Tonglet and paediatric nurse Araceli Castellano, who were raped while camping by three men over the course of several hours one August night in 1974 in the Calanque de Morgiou near Marseille. The men's own lawyers described them as 'pathetic' and pleaded crass stupidity in their defence.[6] In the early hours of the morning, after a night of horror, the two women made straight for the police station to report the crime and then went to the hospital for medical checks and the gathering of evidence. The three perpetrators were soon arrested, much to their surprise, apparently. They admitted to having sex with the women, but claimed it was consensual. The female examining magistrate interviewed the plaintiffs and, in her report, mentioned that they were gay, seemingly in an underhand attempt to discredit them. Through leading questions, she got the women to 'acknowledge' that some of their reactions that night could have misled their attackers into believing they had consented. What actually happened was that, paralysed with fear after being threatened and hit when they initially resisted, they put up no further resistance in the hope that their ordeal would be over as quickly as possible. In the light of the examining magistrate's investigation, the rape charge was downgraded to assault and battery and the men were tried at a magistrate's court – in between somebody who had written a bad cheque and someone who had set fire to a dustbin. At worst, the men faced a one-year suspended prison sentence. This is when the sheer courage of the two women began to shine through, despite the depression, the insomnia and the subsequent ordeals – Araceli had to have an abortion and Anne, whose 'unnatural' sexual preferences were now common knowledge, faced being refused a permanent post as a teacher. And all the while, the men who had raped them were hanging out with their friends and enjoying life.

In the early 1970s, it was rare for women to even report a rape as they were well aware that, in addition to the initial trauma, they were going to have to endure a legal process that, from the moment they went to the police station onwards, would be characterised by suspicion, disdain, sarcasm and endless questions that would implicitly cast aspersions on their integrity. 'But what were you doing out at that time *on your own*? What were you wearing? Did you not consent *to some degree*? Did you *genuinely* struggle?'

And so on. It was as if the victims bore the shame of the act rather than those who had perpetrated it. But, on this occasion, the women stood their ground. Not only did they report the rape but they battled for the case to be heard before a criminal court with a jury. They were backed by feminist collectives, who campaigned to dismantle prejudices and change attitudes, condemning the tolerance of rape as the perpetuation of male domination. They also highlighted the mental repercussions: ruined lives, long-term depression and chronic shame.

Under pressure, the magistrate's court in Marseille ultimately ruled on 15 October 1975 that the case should be referred to the *cour des assises* (a regional court that tries more serious crimes, generally with a jury). Meanwhile, the involvement of Gisèle Halimi proved to be decisive. Impressed by the courage of the two women and moved by their story, she set out to turn the trial of the rapists into a game changer (as she had previously done in Bobigny for abortion) by securing media coverage, mobilising feminist associations and getting leading figures from the worlds of politics, academia, science and culture to appear in court.

The trial took place in an electric atmosphere. On one side were the locals, who had come to support the rapists and were full of threats and invective. On the other were the feminist campaigners vociferously displaying their support and the political and literary celebrities, such as Françoise Mallet-Joris and Arlette Laguiller, who were called by the defence. The president of the court did not in fact allow them to testify on the grounds that this was about trying three individuals accused of raping two young women and not about passing judgement on this type of crime in the abstract. But Gisèle Halimi and her fellow lawyer Agnès Fichot did succeed in confronting French society with its contradictions, blind spots and hypocritical attitudes. The rapists, who, right to the end, claimed to be the victims of injustice and lies, received heavy sentences on 3 May 1978 in Aix-en-Provence, and in December 1980, a new rape law was passed containing a more precise and at the same time broader definition of the crime.[7] Revisiting the affair twenty years later, Anne Tonglet declared: 'In 1978, my rape trial shifted the burden of shame onto the other side for the first time.'[8]

Six years later, another woman came to the fore in the fragile but determined person of Éva Thomas. She appeared without hiding her face on a flagship TV programme of the time called *Les Dossiers de l'écran* to present her book *Le Viol du silence*,[9] an account of the incest that she had endured at the age of fifteen. She began by saying, 'I'm speaking out to dispel the shame.'

Both these affairs are quite old now and, in a sense, dated. It is impossible today to imagine, as was the case at the trial in Aix-en-Provence, victims being insulted and called dykes and sluts, their friends and families receiving death threats and their lawyers being manhandled. In the case of incest, it is equally hard to imagine, as was the case in the 1986 TV programme, doctors being allowed to get away with positing two types of incest: the pathological and devastating kind, and the happy and consensual kind. One might think we live in an age of social awareness and accountability where crimes of this nature have once and for all been recognised for what they are.

And yet ...

The most recent publications on the subject of rape and incest paint the same picture: The number of sexual assaults and cases of incest shows no signs of falling.[10] Reporting these crimes remains problematic and the judicial outcome uncertain, with judges still equally likely to downgrade rapes to sexual assaults on the grounds that the *cour d'assises* is slow, arduous and brutal. A series of scandals have made the headlines in recent years (Harvey Weinstein, Jeffrey Epstein, Dominique Strauss-Kahn, Olivier Duhamel) that have each brought to light a frightening tally of victims, who had until then been suffering in painful, terrible silence. And one cannot help thinking that nothing has changed: There is still that same old unspoken shame haunting them.

Take two recent examples. Sidney Amiel was a respected lawyer and head of a prestigious law firm in Chartres who, in 2017, was accused of a string of sexual assaults against colleagues stretching over several years. One of the victims who testified, some fifteen years after she left the firm, explained her long silence thus: 'Silence is so comfortable. For your friends and family, rape is a taboo subject. It's dirty, you feel shame and disgust.'[11]

The former rugby player Sébastien Boueilh was raped every Friday night by his cousin's husband throughout his adolescence. He eventually went to the police eighteen years later when he found out that he was not the only victim, and his rapist was jailed in 2013. He later stated: 'The feeling I had was one of shame.'[12]

The rationale behind shame and the roots of silence do not coincide exactly when it comes to rape and incest. Rapes are often one-off episodes that are brutally abrupt, and the overwhelming majority of victims are women. It is a single life-shattering moment, though, of course, cases exist of paedophilia – in sporting, teaching or religious contexts, for example – where pre-adolescent boys and girls are repeatedly raped over long periods. Incest tends to involve young children being sexually abused by a father or a stepfather, and it is often recurrent. The aggressor is known: They are the parent, the relative, *the supposed guardian and protector*.

It is possible to identify two reasonably distinct shame-inducing scenarios. On the one hand, there is the shame that arises from a supposed *consent* that is socially (phallocratically) constructed, with rape being a prime example. On the other, there is the shame arising from the silence maintained by the family in the case of incest. Though it goes without saying, of course, that incest also poses the question of consent, and rape the question of silence.

In order for their suffering to be acknowledged and their attacker to be punished, rape victims have to contend with and surmount at least four contiguous walls, forming what one might call a phallocratic enclosure. They are, in turn, a sexual myth, a moral postulate, an archaic social categorisation, and a very strict definition of rape.

The sexual myth shoring up these walls is the male/female opposition, which is conceived of in active and passive terms. This is not restricted to simple anatomy, but extends to supposedly gendered experiences of pleasure and disgust. In the case of women, the pleasure is characterised by relinquishment and passivity – Freud went so far as to talk of masochism as an 'expression of the feminine nature'.[13] In the case of men, according to the founding father of sexology Havelock Ellis, the pleasure is one of conquest and capture. It is a kind of hunting instinct, with women supposedly playing the role of *obliging* prey (though he did also hazard the remark that 'women only feel themselves tenderly loved when they are badly treated by their husbands'[14]). In short, male sexuality is 'naturally' impulsive and aggressive. The male affords (imposes?) the (his?) pleasure and the female receives and gives in to it. One takes (sexual) pleasure in dominating, and the other in being dominated.

These opposing poles (active/passive, male/female, yin/yang, public/private, and so on) are important as they stand, but when they are reversed, or rather combined, they can have an even more decisive impact, as when an active principle is ascribed to female sexuality and a passive disposition to male sexuality. Doctors and priests have long characterised female sexuality as voraciously passive – a chasm furiously demanding to be filled. It is not merely a void or a cavity but a lust that devours. Female passivity is feigned, misleading and a contradiction in terms: In truth, women are lustful temptresses. One finds the accusation of lustfulness – of an insatiable and exhausting demand for sexual pleasure – in Doctor de Bienville's treatise on the *furor uterinus*,[15] which appeared in 1789 but was part of a much older tradition. As for the temptress charge, that can be traced back at least as far as Tertullian, who described women as the 'doorway of the devil'.[16] Their passivity is a trap: With their simpering ways, they insidiously attract men like magnets. In this phallocratic myth, it is men who become the innocent prey. Their sexual activity is classified as reactive, and their sexual impulsiveness is passive in the sense that it is triggered by the woman. On this view of sexual arousal, they are the victims. Women necessarily consent to the sexual act because it is they who bring it about in the first place through the 'violence of their charms', in Rousseau's phrase.[17]

The moral postulate is that of modesty, which is culturally constructed as one of the eternal female traits. But modesty is ambiguous in that one cannot be entirely sure what it conceals. On one interpretation, the reserve which leads a woman to conceal her nudity for as long as possible can be taken to indicate that her body *belongs to her*: that she has an inalienable right to keep it intact, defend her integrity and resist any intrusion. In other words, modesty is the expression of her right to say no. But there is a second, entirely phallocratic interpretation which asserts that a woman's modesty hides not her nudity but her desire. For reasons of social convention (in order not to acquire a reputation as 'easy') or as part of an underhand strategy (resisting in order to arouse desire), she refuses and defends herself to a certain degree, but these are in fact forms of *deferred or disguised consent*. Ultimately, she wanted it all along, enjoyed it and consented to it. Her consent after the fact is deduced from the accomplishment of the act itself, though it initially takes the form of a refusal.

And then there is the archaic social categorisation that involves relegating a woman to the status of a man's 'property' once she is married. If she is single, then she is a piece of merchandise on display, there to be taken. Providing it does not interfere with the bloodline or muddy the waters of inheritance, rape is no more than a response to all this unclaimed property.[18] This social categorisation means that consent is assumed if the raped woman is not married: The phallocratic system insinuates that, by venturing out into the public space unaccompanied, she was being imprudent and placing herself in danger. Her foolhardiness implicitly equates to consent to what befalls her ('Don't be surprised afterwards if …').

One might be tempted to conclude that rape is justified in general in the phallocratic world, but things are actually more complex. Rape continues to be strongly condemned and severely punished, but only if it complies with a very strict six-point definition: The victim must be a married woman; the rapist must be a total stranger (ideally a poor person, an immigrant or a mentally ill individual); the act must occur in an out-of-the-way place (dark alleyway, underground car park, cellar); it must be a sudden, completely unanticipated attack; the victim must put up a heroic though ultimately futile fight (with muffled screams and so on); and there must be an obvious physical threat (such as a knife). This strict definition (the stereotypical rape scenario) automatically excludes the forms of 'consent' so far cited: The element of surprise short-circuits any game of seduction centred around the passive–active dialectic (no a fortiori consent); the elements of constraint and resistance are so pronounced that any modesty or desire games are also ruled out (no a posteriori consent); and since a married woman is involved, who thus belongs to someone else, the rape is immediately recast as theft (hence no consent by definition).

If a woman's experience should stray from this stereotypical scenario (a rape that is accepted as such and so will automatically elicit the compassion of mature men of high status), then the phallocratic system will deploy its agents (police officers, investigators, judges) to insinuate her triple consent (a fortiori, a posteriori, implicit). But only a tiny minority of cases fall into this category. In the overwhelming majority, the rapist is known to the victim (an acquaintance, a colleague, and so on), the rape takes place in a private space, and sheer fear paralyses the victim, who (in a defence mechanism well known to neuropsychologists) enters a state of dissociation and puts up no further resistance, her complete passivity affording a mental refuge from what she is enduring. There again, this stereotypical scenario is not intended to be descriptive or representative – it serves rather to maximise the chances of demonstrating that the victim gave her consent.

And this notion of triple consent – a social and cultural construct – engenders her shame. The torturous line of questioning of investigators and lawyers and the private nature of some of their questions (rape is the only crime where victims' moral probity is placed under the spotlight) all tend towards the same conclusion. If her case does not conform to the stereotype – if, for example, she is a single woman who knew her attacker and had even allowed herself to be courted – then the insinuation is 'Ultimately, you were asking for it.'

Returning to the Aix-en-Provence trial, one can see this attitude pushed to its absolute extreme in the problematic arguments advanced by the defence lawyers (and which are also to be found in political philosophy): *Survival is equated to consent*, this being the common thread running through the three forms of 'consent' we have been describing.[19]

To recap, the two terrified young women, feeling isolated and powerless, let the three attackers into their tent and were soon focused on one thing only: getting them to leave as soon as possible. Paralysed by shock, they stopped resisting while desperately hoping the men would go away. They even tried to elicit their compassion, attempting to engage them in conversation and acting 'friendly' in the hope of taking the edge off the violence.

The lawyers of the three men seized on what was purely a self-preservation strategy and insidiously sought to twist the meaning of the associated vocabulary: The women 'decided' to let it happen, they 'preferred' not to put up a fight, and they ended up 'accepting' the repugnant sexual acts inflicted on them. Their strategy was to shoehorn in a notion of free choice: Did the verbs *to decide, prefer* and *accept* not imply consent? The line of argument went thus: 'At a certain point, you did indeed end up saying yes and ceasing to put up a fight. We grant you that this was a ruse born out of fear, but surely you must admit that such an attitude could be misinterpreted, that you may have *given the impression* of consenting. How is a man supposed to correctly interpret the situation, particularly if they are a bit intellectually challenged, like these three losers?'

What the lawyers were deliberately trying to ignore, of course, was that all this deciding, preferring and accepting was, at root, prompted by panic and a terror of dying, and that there were no grounds for attributing to the women any form of willing participation or freedom of choice. One does not 'consent' to survive. When threatened, it is never a case of 'preferring' life to death. One finds dodges, deploys strategies and ruses, takes snap decisions and resigns oneself to one's fate, but none of this is consent or an expression of free will. No more so than a worker, as Marx pointed out, can be said to be 'free' in accepting a pittance of a wage – they have no choice if they are to survive and feed their children.

Certain political philosophers have also ended up articulating this monstrous notion that survival equates to consent in their efforts to justify obedience to the state. Hobbes is a classic social contract philosopher in that he posits an act of unanimous consent – a rational and freely arrived at choice to live communally – that originally gave birth to a sovereign public authority. In chapter 20 of *Leviathan*, he addresses the question of territorial conquest and colonies: Should one regard the colonising authority as illegitimate and obedience to it as purely the product of violence? Hobbes's answer is categorical and terribly blunt: absolutely not. Both 'commonwealths of institution' (based on unanimous and explicitly articulated consent) and 'commonwealths of acquisition' (involving the subjugation of a people by pure violence) ultimately rest on the same foundations, except that in the second case, the consent is implicit.[20] If the native inhabitants of the territory are still alive, *it means that they've consented*. But does it really make any sense to speak of consent when it has been extracted through violence? To this objection, Hobbes introduces an alarming distinction: It goes without saying that in already existing political societies, coercion is incompatible with consent, which by definition means choosing freely without any force being involved. But things are different in the case of the original act of political consent, which is inextricably tied up with not dying.

Men subject themselves to a sovereign ... This should be noted by those who hold that all covenants are void that proceed from fear of death or violence. If this were true, then no one in any kind of commonwealth would be obliged to be obedient.[21]

This notion of forced consent rears its head when one is attempting to justify unconditional political obedience to the state or to blame a woman who offers no resistance to her rapist. The point, both in the case of the citizen subjugated by the authoritarian state and the woman who has been raped, is to undermine their status as helpless victims: *In some sense* they did indeed consent *because they are still alive.*

This monstrous concept can work its effects in the real world – it is heard on the lips not only of some of the greatest political thinkers but also of rapists and their lawyers. In his closing argument in Aix-en-Provence, the defence lawyer François Tubiana hazarded an odd – and cruel – comparison to express his scepticism as to the reality of the alleged rape. Given that they had talked to the men and acceded to their demands (masturbation, fellatio), could these two young Belgian women really claim to have put up a fight for the entire night like Monsieur Seguin's goat?[22]

It was a vile comparison, and not only because of the implicit suggestion that this is what you got if, like these two women, you dared to free yourself of social conventions. The real point was that it was the little goat's death that proved that it had genuinely tried to resist the wolf. Young ladies, if you survive a so-called rape in one piece, we are entitled to raise an eyebrow.

Because we're wearing miniskirts, and one of us has green hair and the other orange, we must 'fuck like rabbits' and so the rape they are carrying out is not actually a rape ... Three of them with a gun, against two girls they'd beaten to the point of drawing blood: not rape. Because if we'd really been determined not to get raped we would either have preferred to die, or managed to kill them ... If it ended up happening, then the girl must at some level have consented. Never mind if they had to hit her, threaten her, get several guys to hold her down; never mind if she was crying before, during and after ... The very fact that I survived undermines my case.[23]

In defending the two women in court, Gisèle Halimi hit the nail on the head when she exclaimed: 'Just how much and for how long does a woman have to resist being raped? Are you really saying she has to fight to the death?' And she hazarded her own comparison, which emphatically trumped the insidious reference to Alphonse Daudet and his goat:

Members of the jury may be aware that when the Gestapo resorted to torture, some Resistance heroes – yes, heroes – talked. Now who here would dare suggest that by talking, after being violently tortured, they had somehow consented to the regime of their torturers, that they had collaborated?[24]

It is often said, and with good reason, that speaking out is liberating and redemptive – a first step in rebuilding one's life. Silence, by contrast, is the fuel on which incest feeds. In the short term, it keeps it secret; in the long term, it excuses it (why did they not say anything?). Incest inverts intuitive expectations: It is precisely because it is so serious, distressing and destructive (though it also creates a system of power relations, as we will see) that people do not speak about it.

What prevents incest survivors from speaking out for so long?

Fear is doubtless the primary reason. The perpetrator is likely to shut them up with dire threats and emotional blackmail: 'If you say anything ...' And the child trembles in silence, fearing reprisals if they dare tell anyone. But this is not the only source of apprehension: There is also the fear of not being believed. As they do not understand what is happening to them, they do not have the words to describe it. And who would believe them anyway, if they themselves can hardly believe it? How on earth to articulate it, name it, express it? A lot of victims go through this: It is only at the police station when they report it (if they do so early enough) that they learn the word for what has happened to them. The child immediately senses that it is a deviant and unspeakable act. Silence enables them to relegate the catastrophe to sporadic occurrences shrouded in secrecy, outside of which they try to lead a 'normal' life despite the fatigue and sense of emptiness. 'If I talk', they say to themselves, 'the catastrophe will spread to everything, sweeping up everything in its path: family, school and friends. My daily life, where I can still create fragile moments of happiness, will collapse. Nobody will love me any more and I will lose everything.' Any order in the world – family meals, sport at school – rests on the tacit extension of that pact of silence between aggressor and victim, the latter having been duly warned: If you talk, *your world will descend into chaos*, and it will be your fault. It will be a terrible betrayal of your nearest and dearest, you will cause your mother a lot of suffering, you will tear apart your family, and you will sully everyone around you with your indiscretion. *It will all have been down to you.* From such a prospect a survival strategy emerges: Confine the chaos and destruction of everything to oneself, to a devastated private sphere, to a ravaged realm of one's inner being. Seen in this light, the victim's silence becomes terribly heroic: It is not only their way of maintaining order in the world but also of *protecting others* and continuing to be worthy of their love.

Above and beyond the effects of fear, silence can also be the result of an emotional disconnection from language. In some cases, direct threats and emotional blackmail are almost ancillary in their impact compared to the *psychological hold* over the victim. This denotes a form of power (in its primary sense of a capacity to make somebody behave in a way they would not have done otherwise) that is exercised without recourse to duress, violence, rational persuasion or negotiation (but is distinct from classic forms of authority to which we naturally defer). A psychological hold is more akin to an insidious and terribly effective mental *occupation* of the other. To be under that hold is to be deprived of autonomy and inner sovereignty; it is to be governed by another person, as if under the influence of a narcotic. But it is not solely a question of something being stripped away or confiscated. It is an occupying, colonising force. My desires, intentions and thoughts have been overrun, and now I desire and speak *according to somebody else's will.* The victim of incest no longer has their own voice, and their silence is a consequence of this occupation of their voice. Their private space is occupied. The private self emerges out of those moments when I explore and test the contours of my being and have a sense of belonging to myself. Strong emotions, reveries, cherished possessions, one's own body, flights of fantasy, games, whispered things: I establish a nimble familiarity with myself, I learn to inhabit my body and my desire and to give them substance. It is a process of appropriating oneself and constructing a distinct and private self.

In cases of incest, whether it is in my bed at night, alone in my bedroom or in the bath, these private moments become sources of anxiety and potential opportunities for intrusion (*Is he going to suddenly appear?*). The child is dispossessed of those moments when they appropriate their own body, desires and voice and develop an affinity with themselves, constructing an emotional kernel that consolidates and demarcates a 'self as subject' (in the sense that Merleau-Ponty speaks of a body as subject). Their private space is now *occupied* by another person in the same way as we speak of occupied territories: deprived of their sovereignty and under external control. My own pleasure is contaminated by the satisfaction of foreign pleasures, and I have the anguished feeling that my body has been colonised and intruded upon. Penetration, molestation, fingering. The child is also ordered to do things like stroke and lick. There may be no assault and battery, or screaming, but this devastation of their private space is nevertheless fundamentally violent. The reaction will take the form of concealed tears, problematic relationships with other people, an anguished sense of emptiness and a destructive self-disgust. In the fabric of 'ordinary' existence, of 'normal' everyday life, the silence will create dark abscesses, painful swellings and tumours that ultimately ruin an existence – the child will continue to go through the daily motions (the silence means that they can still get up in the morning, do their homework, eat), but the way in which they relate to these things has been poisoned.

The silence of incest is a shameful silence. Firstly, because the abusive act, even if the adult attempts to dress up their monstrous behaviour in words of tenderness or talk of 'trust', is immediately felt by the child or young teenager to be abnormal, out of line and ultimately dirty. Aspects of mature sexuality and adult desire, shot through with pornographic fantasies, force themselves onto a fluid child's sexuality; disturbing and incomprehensible acts leave their emotionally fraught imprint. The child is impregnated with odours and sensations that are immediately experienced as alien and repellent. They sense that 'this isn't right' but they just do not want to take the risk, in talking about it, of disgusting their friends or angering their mother – of sullying others with the stain that now inhabits their inner being. Sometimes they may also tell themselves that they 'should have' done something (put up a fight, said no, spoken out). Their inability to do so, their passivity, can leave them feeling they were at fault for 'doing something silly' – they are ashamed of their own weakness and powerlessness. And, perhaps even more frequently, they may feel ashamed of seeking to please and of continuing to love their father or stepfather even in the midst of all the horror, and hoping that this love will be reciprocated if they go along with it all. It can be a contradictory, unstable and bitter mix of emotions that courses through the child, who may, despite everything, remain attached to their attacker, even if they are traumatised by the price they have to pay for this love. And, finally, as Ferenczi points out in 'Confusion of Tongues', a child's mind is sponge-like and vulnerable to suggestion.[25] This permeability is accentuated by the child's state of shock – as discussed earlier in connection with rape, the brain 'short-circuits' and consciousness becomes dissociated from what the victim is enduring – the soul disconnects from the body. The initial emotional intensity (anxiety, apprehension, fear) of the acts of incest renders the child lastingly suggestible, and shame is the price they pay for this: The abject actions of the perpetrator are translated into an abject self-image and violence against themselves or others (or thoughts of such acts that present as an OCD subtype).

Ultimately, the fact that all of this *really has happened to me* is the principal source of shame. Silence maintains an element of uncertainty, relegating the episodes of sexual abuse to a nebulous semi-reality that is easier to endure. When in the safety of company (at school, at mealtimes and when playing sport), these episodes have the slightly unreal quality of nightmares or delirium. Talking about them would brutally endow them with reality, both in the eyes of others and from one's *own* perspective. Rather than writing them off as 'difficult moments', the child would have to confront them in all their unbearable reality, as well as dealing with the jagged edges of other people's words and the glint of daggers in their eyes. But can something really be said to exist if you never talk about it? I am going to *keep it to myself*. It is obviously a disastrous solution – explosive and destructive – for the child, who is forced to dissociate and split themselves in two, but it strikes them as the *only possible* option. It can therefore be both brutal and comforting for them to discover that they were not the only victim. Brutal, because if others endured it too, it proves that it all really happened. Comforting, in that it shows that he was the sick one, not me.

The purpose of this cruel silence is to legitimise, sanction, shore up and ultimately validate this *raw power*. One could also use the terms *male domination*, *patriarchal power* or *phallocracy*, but I have opted for *raw power* to denote a phenomenon that involves appropriation (the child is the perpetrator's thing, a possession to be used and abused) and a one-way power relation between the dominant and dominated parties, the penetrator and the penetrated, the perpetrator and the victim of incest. A power that ultimately reduces the other to a perpetually available and disposable object – they are made to feel like a worthless piece of junk. I call this form of power 'raw' because no explanation or justification is given for it; there is no pretension to govern or to guide behaviour, and no appeal to a higher source of legitimacy. Rather, it is a power that revolves entirely around the pleasure of possessing an object. *Fructus*: I take from that object what I want, I use and abuse it as I see fit, and I deform it according to my whims. It can scarcely be said to be an abuse *of* power in that abuse is inherent to this form of power – in fact, power in this context is synonymous with abuse. And the victim of this abuse cannot help but feel ashamed since they are reduced to the status of an object *exposed* to the desire of the other and there to be consumed. The nakedness of the child is no longer private – something that they have physically appropriated for themselves in secret – but public, offered up to the gaze of the perpetrator who, from their position of power, exercises their right to inspect and examine. As Levinas observed, shame is the 'radical impossibility of fleeing oneself to hide from oneself'.[26] I am offered up to view and paralysed by my sheer visibility – a frozen object on display.

Incest is shrouded in silence – a layer of concealment like a fog that invades every nook and cranny. But is this shroud not in a sense the apparel of raw power? Is it not possible to detect in this silence a sort of *background hum*? This would equate to the terrible realisation, in certain cases, that sisters have been enduring the same thing (and also keeping quiet), that mothers were aware of what was happening and saying nothing, that brothers had simply shrugged. Nobody says anything, but there is an ambiguity in this silence: Are people not saying anything because it is all too unbearable or because it *goes without saying*? Can it be that nobody is talking about it, but everyone is doing it? Raw power is precisely this intolerable thing that *goes without saying*. It is generative of silence both as its bedrock and its exercise, its precondition and its mode of existence, its basic requirement and its natural element. Shame is its signature marker. That said, this silence is a long learning curve for the victims. Girls will often say that they almost hold it against their mothers more, because their silence seemed to contain a moral lesson: Accept it, because you cannot win by resisting in any case. Suffer in silence just as you do the bullying of the boys at school, or the sexist jokes and inappropriate physical contact that you will have to endure in the workplace; accept your status as the eternal loser, forever inferior and subjugated. A system that brings us to *accept* violence is almost more intolerable than violence itself.

By keeping silent, people manage to grow up. Victims of incest and other forms of abuse also keep quiet because they have built their lives in and on this silence. In the strategies they have developed for maintaining it, and in the permanent secrecy associated with it, they have found a subjective resource for relating to others. Silence thus becomes self-perpetuating: I will keep silent because I have already kept silent for so long. This silence is now my foundation stone. It is similar to cases of serious physical injury where bodies reconfigure their whole way of moving so as not to overly solicit the sensitive zones – it is a pain-avoidance strategy. In due course, when such a body walks, sits down, greets you or stretches out its arms, it does so in a *style* that carries the imprint of the initial injury. In the same way, existences reconfigure themselves around a sense of shame and a painful silence, which have become the catastrophic cornerstone of these scarred lives – the central chaos around which their sources of pleasure, their friendships and their life choices orbit. Speaking of her rape, Virginie Despentes confides:

> I always imagine that one day I will be done with it. Will have got over the event: emptied it, exhausted it. Impossible. It is a founding event. Of who I am as a writer, and as a woman who is no longer quite a woman. It is both that which disfigures me, and that which makes me.[27]

Is it possible that this silence about raw power is the foundation not only of the individual but of society as a whole? Marx placed appropriation at the heart of his system, as an anthropological process that was elemental and fundamental. To work is to shape, transform and appropriate nature. To live is also to appropriate: to appropriate one's body and also one's environment to make it a reflection of oneself, a source of security and a place where one feels at home (what the Stoics called *oikeiôsis*). To appropriate oneself is to create a self and a world that are recognisable, reassuring and distinctly one's own. One might call this an ethical appropriation.

But there also exists a capitalist mode of appropriation, according to Marx, that involves the occupation and violation of that which belongs to others (their labour power, the time they have to themselves, their presence in the world, their inner existence, and so on), the alienation of their existence and the unbridled exploitation of the great mass of *diminished* men and women. This abusive form of appropriation that involves 'disappropriating' others is raw power. The core aim of the political system is to institutionalise it through the hallowed legal concept of private property, which can be defined as a guaranteed right to use and abuse.

And the sense of the great struggles and collective revolts, as well as of the personal combats and individual odysseys, can be expressed as a quest for 'reappropriation': to reappropriate for ourselves the means of production and overcome the alienation of labour, to reappropriate a private space that has been ravaged by adult male desire and to reappropriate identities stolen by colonial ideology.[28] The true struggles are not about conquest but reappropriation.

The political system, with its prolix laws and eloquent founding principles, *contains* raw power. It contains it in the sense that riverbanks contain the river, to use Hobbes's metaphor. In other words, the system places constraints on it but at the same time ensures that it exists; it keeps it well concealed, though this raw power is actually its beating heart. It is the kernel of our socio-political constructions, *the thing that is always taken as read*, just as the state is something that has always already been consented to, according to Hobbes. Incest, rape and ill-treatment are the sharp splinters that emanate from it, its expressive monads. They are total social facts that reflect the nature of the system. What we call the system of male domination, the patriarchy or the phallocracy is the symbolic institutionalisation of raw power. And shame is the emotional marker of its acceptance. Virginie Despentes once again captures this in typically pithy fashion:

> The female condition, its code. Forever guilty of what is done to us. Creatures held responsible for the desire we provoke. Rape is a well-defined political strategy: the bare bones of capitalism, it is the crude and blunt representation of the exercise of power.[29]

What we call the taboo of incest does not pertain to not practising it – incest is unfortunately too widespread to be credibly presented as a towering taboo. The only real transgression is to speak of it. And it is this code of silence that is the enabler of raw power.

7

The Sexual Foundations of the Republic

It all began with a nagging suspicion and perhaps a hint of one-upmanship. My goal here is to reconstruct the founding myth of the Roman Republic, drawing on fragments from Livy, Ovid, Dionysius of Halicarnassus, William Shakespeare and André Obey (all men!) to weave an idealised narrative and reveal the beating dramatic heart of this legend that has inspired poets, playwrights, moral philosophers and musicians.[1] First scene: We need to imagine a small group of young aristocratic commanders conducting a siege. But the town of Ardea is so far holding out, and so they drink to overcome their boredom and their yearning for Rome. There are three key figures among these revellers. Collatinus is a fine figure of a man with excellent breeding: a happily married man, a loyal friend and a good soldier. He ticks all the boxes, including those of dullness. He is essentially the 'husband figure'. Then there is the Etruscan prince Tarquin, the son of the king, who spends much of his time whoring. A quarrelsome, tyrannical and capricious brute, he takes pleasure in using and abusing, possessing and destroying. Nothing will stop him getting what he wants. And the third character is their drinking partner Brutus, seemingly an amiable buffoon, who in fact turns out to be the master of the situation at the climax of the tragedy. It is he who whips the Romans up into revolt against the depraved Etruscan princes.

Alcohol can have an embittering effect, and the conversation soon turns to the men's wives and sisters. What are they up to while we are engaged in battle here in the cold? Spurred on by the wine, according to Livy, the men decide to settle the argument of who has the most virtuous and chaste wife by galloping off to Rome and paying them a surprise visit.

The spectacle they encounter is illuminating. They find one wife in the arms of another man and a second man's sister drunk and feasting like there is no tomorrow. A third woman has deserted the premises and cannot be found. The only ray of light amid all this moral debauchery, the solitary diamond in the darkness, is Collatinus's wife Lucretia, whom they find spinning wool with her maids. It is a celestial vision of a Roman matriarch in all her ravishing splendour and purity of virtue, keeping the household in sound financial and moral order. She is the very symbol of sexual and economic virtue, the two being inextricably entwined. The spectacle of the women in Rome sobers up our three male protagonists. It may be that a self-satisfied Collatinus indulges in a little bragging, but, for Tarquin, it is a threefold assault on his body and mind. This has nothing to do with the sight of the women of lax morals, which is merely a confirmation of his cynical outlook on life. It is the image of Lucretia that completely unhinges him. Firstly, he is incensed by this object that is both desirable and forbidden, by this chastity of the perfect wife (Will she resist me?), as if his omnipotence is called into question by the fact that another man possesses this perfect object (narcissistic shame). Secondly, there is the slight humiliation of the superior who has to endure the bragging of an inferior. Tarquin is forced to ask himself the question: For all my riches and earthly pleasures, have I perhaps been missing out all along? Look at this couple – a beautiful and loving woman and a very happy husband, who is a good friend and an accomplished soldier (social-ideal shame). And, thirdly, could it be that Tarquin has been overcome by an irresistible desire? Not merely jealousy or envy, but pangs of love at the sight of this face and body: the ivory white of her shoulders and the blood red of her lips, the interplay of red and white that Shakespeare sings the praises of. The men return to their tents to sleep, but Tarquin remains awake, his heart beating uncontrollably. And this is when the decision is taken: I am returning to Rome. The following evening, he gallops there again, but this time his haste and desperation seem to silence his conscience and eradicate his scruples.

Scene Two. Tarquin arrives in Rome late in the evening. He goes to Lucretia's home, claims his horse is lame and asks to stay the night. Questions of moral propriety intrude even at this point: Is it decent, is it the done thing, for a woman at home alone to allow a man to stay when her husband is far away? But would it not be even more improper to refuse hospitality to a powerful man who is also the brother-in-arms of one's spouse?

In the end, the prince is allocated a bedroom, and night falls. Night protects; it is the natural element of sexual modesty. What is clothing after all but the veil of night on naked skin? The skull, for its part, is a cave of shadows in which shameful thoughts are sealed behind the door of the lips. Night conceals, its darkness harbouring that which does not belong in broad daylight.

In Racine's eponymous play, Phaedra keeps to the shadows and avoids the light. What strange affliction has beset the daughter of the sun that she is unwilling to show herself in the light of day?

The answer is that she is ashamed of her raging desire for her stepson Hippolytus. Racine makes a clear distinction between shame and guilt. One feels guilty about what one has done or allowed to happen – the regrettable ways in which one has exercised one's freedom. But one does not feel responsible for one's desires, as Racine states in the preface: The drives of his heroine are not an expression of her will, and she is not a martyr to guilt. We are however ashamed of what we can feel bubbling up and groaning inside us like a monstrous alien presence ('O you who see to what shame I have come, implacable Venus').[2] Desire is always an aberrant Other within us, bellowing its demands. We feel ashamed of hosting this monstrosity that escapes our grasp, overwhelms us, drives us to distraction and defines us.

This is also Saint Augustine's interpretation of humanity's expulsion from heaven on earth in Genesis. In Book XIV of *The City of God*, he shows how the original emotion is one of shame: When Adam and Eve become aware of each other's nudity, they suddenly feel an irrepressible desire and arousal that immediately finds physical expression. Sexuality does exist in paradise, but it is a sexuality without desire. The sanction for our original sin, together with death, illness and suffering, is sex, which is to say that uncontrollable part of ourselves that absolutely refuses to obey us. Adam and Eve can neither repress their desire nor control its physical manifestations (an erection, heart palpitations, and so on). And, as they are expelled from paradise, this is what they are ashamed of: As soon as they cross the threshold and become aware of their nudity, desire is brutally awakened in them, taking them by surprise and confusing and unsettling them. From now on, they (and we) will just have to live with the shame associated with the sex component of our sexual identity. A shame that derives first and foremost from the fact that it is outside of our

control and defies our sovereignty, and also because it is writ large
and unequivocally on our bodies, clear for all to see. For having
disobeyed, Adam and Eve are punished through this completely
unruly sex drive, which is in itself the epitome of disobedience.

> They had shame now where they had none before. They experi-
> enced a new motion of their flesh, which had become disobedient to
> them, in strict retribution of their own disobedience to God.[3]

Night protects, but in dissimulating, it also liberates; it is the time
when desires stir and appetites are whetted. There exists a kind
of blanket of impunity: Can events that happen at night really
be said to exist? As Tarquin stealthily creeps towards the young
bride's bedchamber like a wild cat, there are, nevertheless, brutal
flickers of conscience (What has come over me? What on earth
am I doing here?).

First scene: the failed seduction. 'It's me!' Initially, he hopes to
dazzle and seduce. He talks a lot and, depending on the version
you read, employs a variety of tactics. 'So many women desire
me, and such an offer (of my body) is just too good to pass up.'
He extols the virtues of Epicureanism, claiming that the so-called
chastity of women simply reflects a lack of opportunities. He
promises money and other future rewards if she gives in to him.
He exhorts her to examine her feelings: 'Be honest, behind the
façade of the wife, don't you feel the mutual desire, our magnetic
physical attraction to each other? Don't try to pretend otherwise!'

But nothing works – Lucretia resists and refuses all these
purported pleasures, which would be nothing compared to her
defiled virtue and the betrayal of her husband. Whereupon Tarquin
plays the final ace up his sleeve: the threat of irredeemable shame,

of a stain that will survive her and tarnish all her descendants. 'Very well, but know this: If you turn me down, I will kill you and a slave. I will undress both of you and lay your corpses next to each other in bed. I will tell everybody that I heard noises, found the two of you in adulterous embrace and avenged my friend by slaying you both. The shame is sure to survive you.'

It is at this point that Lucretia finally allows herself to be sexually possessed. She does not surrender in the face of fear, an unsheathed sword or the threat of violence and death. The epitome of fragility exposed and dignity preserved, she does buckle at the thought of something worse than death: a shame that survives her. This then is the rape scene, the resonant centrepiece of the story but also the void at its heart (the rape is never explicitly described) around which everything turns – the before (criminal desire) and the after (righteous anger). His desire satisfied, Tarquin returns to camp in the early hours of the morning and resumes his military duties as if nothing has happened.

Third act: Lucretia awakens (assuming she has got a wink of sleep) from her night of horror. Dead to the world, she feels attacked by the light of day. She is no more than a shadow of herself, and it feels like a persistent fog has come between her and her own self. In Britten's opera, this is the most poignant moment.

Lucretia sends for her father and her husband and conceals a dagger on her person. At the sight of her pale tear-stained face, they assail her with questions and eventually learn from the maids that Tarquin spent the previous night there. They immediately fear the worst, and Lucretia silently confirms their suspicions. Moved to anger, they pledge to avenge her while also seeking to reassure her: 'It is not your fault, you gave in only under duress.' Perhaps sensing her intentions, they insist that her soul remains innocent and that she has nothing to reproach herself for.

She eventually emerges from her silence to pronounce her own sentence against herself: 'I am innocent of fault, but I will take my punishment. Never shall Lucretia provide a precedent for unchaste women to escape what they deserve.'[4] She does not die of shame; on the contrary, dying is her only way of eradicating shame.

There has been much debate as to Lucretia's motives – objective and subjective – for committing suicide.[5] The 'objective' reason most often advanced is that she felt sullied by the forced sexual encounter. Impurity automatically results from it, the rape dragging both parties into the mire and tainting her forever.[6] She has to die, both because she has been polluted by the rape (and has therefore become impure for her husband) and in order to bring about the vengeance that will purify her after her death.

The 'subjective' reason given is that her death serves as proof that she was brutally forced to submit to an act that was utterly repulsive to her – the sheer extremity of her reaction will prevent anyone from trying to claim later that she passed a night of adultery off as a rape.

It is worth citing again the line that Livy gives her: 'I am innocent of fault, but I will take my punishment. Never shall Lucretia provide a precedent for unchaste women to escape what they deserve.' When one thinks about it, this is a terrible thing to say, as if deception is always to be suspected when a woman is raped. Returning to Saint Augustine, in his own interpretation of the Roman myth he airs an even more reprehensible theory (though he then rejects it, the damage has been done):

Or perhaps she is not there, because she slew herself conscious of guilt, not of innocence? She herself alone knows her reason; but what if she was betrayed by the pleasure of the act, and gave some consent to Sextus, though so violently abusing her, and then was so affected with remorse that she thought death alone could expiate her sin?[7]

Lucretia was indeed taken by force, she was indeed raped, concedes Saint Augustine, but maybe she could not help feeling a certain pleasure during the ignoble act, for which she punished herself afterwards.

The final scene of the myth: a group of proud Romans who vow over Lucretia's dead body to avenge her. She is laid out, with her wound still gaping, in the Forum, which prompts a popular uprising, followed by the flight of the Etruscan kings and, ultimately, the creation of a republic.

This myth therefore proposes a sexual genealogy for politics, but a very different one from that advanced by Freud in *Totem and Taboo*, where he argues that political obedience derives from the brothers' guilt at killing the father of the clan. The genealogy proposed by the Lucretia myth is based on shame. Sexual perfection is embodied by the married couple, which, as Paul Veyne reminds us, was a Roman invention.[8] The political meaning of the myth lies in the promise of complementarity, the public and private being two mutually supporting spaces. In order to exercise their public duties with the necessary serenity and vigour, men need the security of an impeccably run household. The myth is saying that it is ultimately women who hold together the republic. Their chastity and propriety underpin the virility of male Roman citizens when they are defending the public good in the Senate or Forum. If the wife allows sexual disorder to reign in the privacy of the home, then the whole system crumbles.

Lucretia is viewed as one of the great heroines of antiquity, but her exalted status is problematic. For a start, it is a decidedly gendered view of the world, allocating fixed domains to men and women and complementary duties to each. But the linchpin of it all is the wife's sexual virtue. Foucault argued that the crucial question in Ancient Greece when assessing a citizen's ability to hold a political post was: 'Is he faithful to his principles?' In other words, is he master of himself? For before one can pretend to govern others, one must be capable of governing oneself.

But the Latin question, when it came to ensuring the future of the republic, was: Is *she* faithful? The wife's sexuality provided the guarantee of the husband's political perfection. For men, justice; for women, shame. That way, the republic would be on sound footing.[9]

8

Aidos

What defines shameless behaviour? An absence of reserve: I flaunt myself, my qualifications, my personality, my success, my private life and my body. I have no shame, as they say. By contrast, shame can denote an ability to put the brakes on and rein oneself in – to display a certain reserve. Is one capable of restraining oneself *through shame* from doing wrong or committing an injustice? This is the secret to ancient Greek ethics, at whose core lies the concept of *aidos*.

These days, it is difficult to imagine shame being an ethical cornerstone, so accustomed are we to viewing it as a repository of bitterness and suffering that needs to be eradicated at all costs – a wound to be healed, a poison to be neutralised. Overcoming shame and rooting out its causes is the stated objective of the purveyors of wellness and happiness. It is as if Nietzsche's aspiration in *The Gay Science* has become our principal ethical injunction: 'Whom do you call bad? Those who always want to put others to shame. What do you consider most humane? To spare someone shame. What is the seal of liberation? No longer being ashamed in front of oneself.'[1] Shame is now essentially condemned as a poison of the soul, the major obstacle to resilience, the worst enemy of happiness – it is what stops us becoming ourselves, reaching our full potential, enjoying the best of life and other people and taking pleasure in being ourselves.

And yet one finds in Confucius and Plato, who, in their respective ways, each set out the spiritual foundations for the close intertwining of ethics and politics, unambiguous statements to the effect that shame is the major ethical component of reserve, communal living and the pursuit of the good:

> The Master said, 'If you guide the people with ordinances and statutes and keep them in line with [threats of] punishment, they will try to stay out of trouble but will have no sense of shame. If you guide them with exemplary virtue [de] and keep them in line with the practice of the rites [li], they will have a sense of shame and will know to reform themselves.'[2]

A sense of shame at acting disgracefully and pride in acting well. Without these, no individual or city can achieve anything great or fine.[3]

What is this shame that is presented as a kind of moral perfection in ancient philosophy?

The idea makes its first appearance in *The Analects* by Confucius (it has been said that never has such a small book had such a strong impact on such a wide public over such a long period).[4] Hegel wrote off the work as insipid, but he evidently failed to grasp that the apparent banality of the statements it contains have the clarity (and depth) of the purest water. There are no juicy paradoxes to delight a brilliant mind and no esoteric utterances to inspire a sophisticated consciousness. There may be rather a lot of platitudinous statements, but their combined effect is dizzying.

It is a collection of sayings that converges towards a single goal: spelling out and thereby encouraging the human virtues which, when cultivated, will result in a harmonious city (a stable social order and collective happiness).[5]

In terms of how we relate to each other, (filial) *piety* is what is needed – this is the virtue that maintains an unbroken connection between contemporaries and their ancestors. It imposes on us a duty of honesty and justice towards others and rests on the feeling that we are eternally indebted. It is a virtue that entails openness and ongoing reciprocation in our relationships with others – in short, it acts as a point of ethical intersection.

In terms of our attitude towards the rules, it is incumbent upon us to be *deferential*: to obey, though not fanatically, and to observe rites, but without hypocrisy. Deference is a frame of mind that might be described as a quiet conviction that by respecting conventions and laws, one is contributing to social order.

And, lastly, when it comes to one's rapport with oneself, *modesty* is called for if we are to avoid being presumptuous. It is a virtue of self-effacement that involves a reining in of the ego. There are no heroes in morality.

What these three human virtues share is a basic sense of humility, restraint and reserve, and this is what is meant by shame in Eastern thinking. It is not so much a virtue among others as a principle that underpins all of them, or rather prevents them from being twisted out of their natural shape through exaggeration, as when excessive generosity tips over into irresponsible extravagance, undue honesty leads to oversharing, or disproportionate deference descends into hypocritical social niceties.

Shame stops these ethical values being deformed, thereby avoiding counterproductive excesses and pointless posturing. We should invariably act just within our capacities, keeping a little moral energy in reserve, just as one curbs natural vigour in order to expend it in a balanced way. Shame introduces a principle of economy into ethics and functions as the continuous bass note of morality. It imposes limits and thereby prevents emotional outbursts, transgressions and people simply doing as they please. An illustration of this would be Confucius's assertion that the wise person 'would be ashamed to let his words run ahead of his action'.[6] He invests more energy in concrete action than verbal fanfare, avoiding attention-grabbing declarations that are really little more than a smokescreen.

Being presumptuous leads to our moral downfall, plunging us into the bottomless chasm of vanity and illusion and divorcing what we say from what we do, our principles from our conduct. The wise person embraces the restraining properties of shame, which ensure that their virtues are not denatured. This ethical privileging of reserve in Eastern thought is not, however, about creating a secret garden of our own. Rather, it is about distinguishing between two different forms of external conduct: the fake façade of noisy self-promotion and the quiet and efficient accomplishment of concrete actions. Shame prompts us to do things rather than boasting about them. It enables us to be genuinely fair, deferential and sincere, rather than wasting all our energies on parading such virtues.

What Confucius expresses in the vocabulary of reserve is approached by Plato through the lens of fear. Different approaches they may be, but shame plays a *restraining* role in both. Plato's conception can be conveyed through two images and two statements.

In *Protagoras*, we find the myth of the foundation of politics: Being naturally vulnerable, mankind receives the gift of fire from

Prometheus so that it can hold its own in the natural world. But a second challenge immediately presents itself: surviving the internal dissensions that could doom humanity to unending and deadly strife. To stave off this threat of extinction, Zeus sends Hermes to distribute shame (*aidos*) and justice (*dikē*)[7] to all people.

In his eulogy of love in *The Symposium*, Phaedrus imagines a perfect army.[8] If you want to create an invincible phalanx, recruit lovers who will fight side by side. They will throw themselves into battle with even greater courage, as they would be ashamed of showing the slightest hint of cowardice in front of their loved one. It is in the context of this martial dream that Plato gives Phaedrus the following lines:

> Neither family bonds nor public status nor wealth nor anything else is as effective as love in implanting something which gives lifelong guidance to those who are to lead good lives. What is this? A sense of shame (*aiskhunê*) at acting disgracefully and pride (*philotimia*) in acting well.[9]

In the *Charmides*, a very early Platonic dialogue, we find the following: 'Sound-mindedness (*sôphrosunê*) makes a human being have a sense of shame (*aiskhunesthai*).' And in the *Laws*, the final dialogue that he wrote in old age, there is this: 'And there is the fear of an evil reputation; we are afraid of being thought evil, because we do or say some dishonourable thing, which fear we and all men term shame (*aiskhunê*).'[10]

Plato ascribes a good deal to shame: It is a facilitator of communal living (*Protagoras*), the essence of sound-mindedness or wisdom (*Charmides*) and a source of courage (*The Symposium*). It is a kind of apprehension, but distinct from the fear we feel in the presence of actual danger. It is more a fear of that which could damage our public image. If I do this or that, what will people say about me? This fear is not born out of cowardice (even though, like cowardice, it inhibits and restrains us) – it has more of an anticipatory quality, which is why ethical shame is always conjugated in the conditional: No, I refuse to do it, *I would be so ashamed if* ... It is a spectre hanging over us, a shame of shame itself: I imagine the shame in advance so that I do not actually have to experience it. I imagine the discredit that a particular decision would bring upon me or the infamy associated with a particular act, and that image disturbs me. We project ourselves into all manner of scenarios beneath the gaze of other people, and those imaginings prompt us to erect a moral barrier.

Such shame-based ethics have come in for a great deal of criticism and have lost ground somewhat to systems based on the notion of personal fault. Three accusations are commonly levelled, the first of which, as we have already seen, involves the conformist dimension of this obsession with other people's opinions: The 'good' becomes synonymous with the socially approved. Virtuous behaviour thus equates to respecting conventions. We refrain from killing our neighbour for the same reason that we do not wipe our nose with our hand in public: It is simply not the done thing.

A second criticism relates to what one might call the aesthetic dimension. The constant thought experiments (How would I be regarded if ...?) that guide our moral choices elevate the *spectacle* that I am likely to make of myself into the decisive criterion. Shame, as Plato points out, is associated with ugly or graceless actions, and pride with beautiful actions.[11] But is morality really about coming across well, being admired and conforming to aesthetic canons? Could it be that we are virtuous out of narcissism or dandyism?

The third criticism is that shame-based ethics seem to involve teaching people a lesson through humiliation. The logic behind them is that carefully orchestrated and memorable public punishments will durably implant shame – in the guilty party, of course, who will forever associate their trespass with a mortifying humiliation, but also in the minds of the spectators, who will be keen to avoid the same fate. This dimension of teaching people a lesson has formed the basis for chilling tales by Karl Philipp Moritz (*Anton Reiser*, 1785), Thomas Bernhard (*Die Ursache*, 1975) and Balzac (*Louis Lambert*, 1832) among others. These coming-of-age stories show how such symbolic humiliations – immediately felt to be gratuitous, unjust and needlessly cruel – do not in fact teach the victims a moral lesson but rather harden their attitudes, while affording onlookers simple schadenfreude. Virtue has never been fashioned out of humiliation.

So, should these shame-based ethics be consigned to history? We certainly still continue to talk about 'shameless' behaviour and we appear to implicitly regret the move away from such ethics when we indignantly exclaim, 'Do people have no shame any more?'

I would point out that the objections set out above apply more readily to decadent, or at least distorted, versions of Greek ethics, namely those that insist on the inner versus outer distinction. It is as if guilt alone is entitled to inhabit the depths of the soul, whereas shame is merely attached to the superficial desire to conform to the norm and obey the rules. People tend to forget, for example, that the opposite of *guilty* is *innocent*, but the opposite of *shameful* is indeed *shameless* – in the latter case, it is the first word that carries the positive ethical value.

But, above all, the criticisms miss what is most essential about these moral propositions: the imaginative dynamic and the appeal to meaningful witnesses. I project myself, I pre-visualise, I anticipate. My imagination is at the helm, fuelling the fear of the spectacle I might make of myself and furnishing images for hypothetical scenarios: *I would be so ashamed if . . .* But in front of whom? Not necessarily in front of society as a whole or people in general. I imagine what a *specific* person, alarmed or disappointed by my behaviour, would think of me and say about me – I introject the severe gaze of a particular third party. And these are all meaningful witnesses because they are respected friends and people who matter to me. The only shame that counts is that which one feels before those one respects and admires – a select minority as opposed to 'everybody else'. Aristotle claims that friendship is a rare thing ('O my friends, there is no friend') which depends on shared values: a friend functions in some sense as a yardstick by which I judge my own choices in life, and I enjoy seeing in my friend an attachment to principles which I strive to live by, too.[12] When our imagination generates its shame scenarios, the question becomes: If I allow myself to do such-and-such thing, am I prepared to endure (even if it is something I am projecting myself) the contempt of my best friend, which would necessarily mean feeling contempt for myself too?

Alcibiades was bold and brash – a young man who was too handsome, ambitious and irrepressible for his own good. A brilliant politician and fearless soldier, he charmed the whole of Athens and notched up one triumph and conquest after another, all the while making enemies and cynically switching sides. He was afraid of nothing, except Socrates:

> He's the only person in whose company I've had an experience you
> might think me incapable of – feeling shame with someone; I only
> feel shame in his company. I'm well aware that I can't argue against

him and that I should do what he tells me; but when I leave him, I'm carried away by the people's admiration. So I act like a runaway slave and escape from him; and whenever I see him, I'm ashamed because of what he's made me agree to.[13]

This ethical shame is self-generated through the thought experiments conducted by my imagination. It is neither an emotion, in the sense of a pitiful feeling that overcomes and overwhelms me, nor a virtue, in the sense of an active moral stance that I adopt on the basis of lived experiences. *Aidos* is a self-generated experience: I nurture it through regular exercises and repeated mental rehearsals in order to shape my ethical rapport with myself.

9

Philosophy as the Great Shamer

To what extent could shame, which regulates our relationship with the good, also regulate our relationship with the true? It might, if we alter the equation slightly: Whereas the wise person invites us to shame *ourselves* through imaginary projections (*aidos* as a mental exercise and the structuring principle of their ethics), the philosopher's aim is more to 'shame' and provoke somebody else (their disciple, interlocutor, and so on).

On several occasions, Pope Francis has spoken of what he calls the 'grace of feeling ashamed' in his homilies.[1] It is a strange expression, as we tend to view shame as consisting of a lot of unjust suffering – a kind of mental scourge or poison. Making it out to be a form of grace – a divine gift – seems rather incongruous (unless, of course, we believe God to be cruel). But his meaning becomes clearer from the context: He is talking about the 'examination of conscience', which requires lucidity, sincerity and absolutely no leniency with oneself. When it comes to sharing things with others, we have a distinct tendency to distance ourselves from the murkier corners of our mind (ugly motivations, abject desires, ignominious memories), precisely to avoid feeling ashamed. But looking the other way traps us in our self-created rut.

Christian spiritual advisers used to set great store by external signs of shame prior to painful confessions. This was the moment to be attentive and tease out a truth, whose presence was betrayed by a certain embarrassment (*erubescentia*) and heavy silences.[2] Shame is always ambiguous. With unpalatable truths, there are, in fact, two distinct phases of discomfort – the fear before speaking and the pain at the moment of speaking – and shame is present at both. It is what prevents us from confessing to them (a repressive force) and also the state in which we find ourselves when we articulate them (the painful disclosure). Asking God for the grace of shame (Lord, please make me ashamed!) is to take things further still. We might feel we need strength to go all the way to the heart of our shame and that the journey will be cleansing if we see it through uncompromisingly. The decision to confront it amounts to a commitment to inner transformation. And this is where the notion of grace comes in, for it can be extremely difficult to completely eradicate the temptation to be lenient on oneself. We feel no need to confess to things of which we are not necessarily ashamed, since we have already found excuses with which to assuage our conscience. This is where we need external assistance, because otherwise it is too easy for us to downplay things ('It's no big deal.'). A properly divine and purifying shame will make me ashamed of what I could have relegated to mere peccadilloes, and will thereby set me on the path to spiritual transformation.

In a more secular but equally insistent vein, in response to his student Theodor Reik, who during a session admitted to not saying what was on his mind out of pure shame, Freud exclaimed: 'Be ashamed, but say it!'[3] The basic rule of psychoanalysis is well known: You describe out loud any thoughts or images that may 'spontaneously' occur to you without seeking to censor the more outlandish or improper ones. In this context, shame is a good sign. Feeling yourself blush as you speak suggests that you are getting closer to the hidden self. You are within touching distance of forbidden truths, and you are hot under the collar.

Well before the advent of psychoanalysis and indeed the Christian examination of conscience, philosophy in its Socratic form had already established a strong connection between speaking the truth and feeling ashamed, proposing a unique and uncompromising model of cathartic shame. Naturally, we also find in Plato's dialogues a number of passages where shame is analysed in a conventional way as an obstacle to the serious pursuit of truth. We should not forget the public dimension to the Socratic jousts: The presence of 'spectators' prompts Socrates' interlocutors to keep to themselves viewpoints that today we would call politically incorrect. They opt instead for vague generalities and consensual opinions that will not shock anyone. We see this in *Gorgias* when the first two sophists, Polus and Gorgias, take up Socrates' challenge of defining rhetoric. They do not quite dare take their argument to its logical conclusion and accept that ultimately a good rhetorician can (must?) be completely amoral in that he is willing to defend the true or the false, the ignoble or the sublime – his only interest is in winning over his audience. When Callicles intervenes to declare unabashedly that rhetoric is nothing but the art of astutely using the resources of language for the purposes of power, Socrates is delighted to have found a worthy interlocutor. You at least, he tells him, are not ashamed to tell me what you think; you speak freely (*parrêsia*), you do not worry about social conventions and you do not suffer from false modesty. You are a man I can debate with.[4]

But what is being talked about here is shame in the weak sense, as a kind of restraint dictated by conventions. Within the framework of a philosophical dialogue, the key thing is to 'cross-examine a man's words, when he thinks that he is saying something and is really saying nothing'.[5] By practising the art of refutation (*elegkhein*: to discuss, raise objections, correct), pressing them with questions and backing them into a corner, Socrates forces his interlocutor to reflect on the *extent to which he thinks what he thinks* or knows what he knows. Philosophy consists precisely of this kind of cross-examination. Prove to me that your knowledge is more than mere rote learning, your convictions more than the accumulated silt deposited by your family and friends, your judgement more than a reflex reaction – prove to me that they are deeply ingrained in your soul because they are the fruit of your own thinking.

By harassing his sparring partner with repeated demands for further precisions, Socrates relentlessly strips him of his defences, leaving him confused and *ashamed*. Confronted with his own contradictions and backed into a corner by his own assertions, he ends up 'angry with himself'.[6] This is an initial positive sign: His anger reflects a disappointment with himself, and this will soon be followed by a salutary and purifying shame. He feels ashamed because his own soul has been laid bare in front of everyone else, stripped of the worthless rags of social and family truths and the scholarly pseudo-knowledge in which it was draped (with which it was adorned, even). And at this point, the soul is liberated and alleviated of the burden of received opinions and grandstanding convictions:

> The purifier of the soul is conscious that his patient will receive no benefit from the application of knowledge until he is refuted, and

from refutation learns modesty; he must be purged of his prejudices first and made to think that he knows only what he knows, and no more.[7]

It is a cathartic shame, and, in this sense, the initial function of philosophy is to shame people. The goal is never, however, to humiliate someone on account of their ignorance (the puerile, dangerous and thoroughly reprehensible type of shaming of our schooldays). Indeed, ignorance can be seen as something of a blessing: a transparent, flexible soul that is not yet covered in the thick silt of the *doxa* or weighed down and hindered by fashionable convictions. A soul that remains lively and light enough to explore its own unexploited resources and mine them for self-produced truths.

In a provocative turning of the tables, philosophy asserts that one can be proud of one's ignorance but ashamed of one's knowledge.

It is the Socratic way: I know that I know nothing. The opposite of truth is not error but the unexamined received opinion. The real enemy is unthinking certainty. Socrates humiliates pretensions to knowledge and socially comforting convictions. And, if philosophy shames, it is because it lays the soul bare – the crumbling of its superficial knowledge leaves it terribly exposed. That said, it can be a perilous exercise: The endlessly enquiring Socrates eventually outstayed his welcome and was condemned to death by Athens. The conceited politicians, arrogant magistrates and pretentious artists did not take kindly to having their souls stripped bare in public.

I see a modern-day heir to this Socratic shaming in Jacques Lacan when he lectured to the young pretenders and future analysts who had come to hear about the unconscious, transference and symptoms, and to glean some cultural capital on the symbolic and the imaginary. Instead, what they got was a good shaming. If one is honest, the experience of reading his *Seminars* is incredibly irritating. It is like grabbing a handful of sand and feeling it running through one's fingers – after a few pages, one's hand is desperately empty. In constructing impossibly complex sentences ridden with discourse markers that seem to contradict the point he is making (as if every apparent assertion is followed by an 'unless the opposite is the case'), he orchestrates a gigantic shaming. Though arrogant souls (remarkably numerous) might emerge from the experience spouting esoteric phrases, what he actually seems to be saying is: If you think you have understood this, you are sorely mistaken. And, if these seminars serve any purpose, it is to divest you of this flimsy semblance of knowledge that you claim to get from me. You would really be very ill-advised to leave here thinking you have understood, that you have got the phrase down in your little grey exercise book and now all you have to do is learn it by heart and then reel it off to others. Are you really wiser than you were yesterday? 'If the reasons for your presence here are not entirely ignoble … then it's because I succeed in shaming you – not too much, but enough all the same.'[8]

Shame is there to preserve his audience from dogma: Believing we know something is so much more dangerous and damaging than ignorance. To see philosophy as an exercise in shaming is to perceive its potential for protecting us (at least to some extent) from foolishness and vulgarity of the mind. The banality of evil is the know-it-all attitude with which some lord it over others, the imbecilic claim to superior knowledge and the attendant contempt of others, and the temptation to flaunt one's qualifications in order to humiliate.

Philosophy's only public function and use is to shame the truth terrorists.

10

Future Imperfect

People can survive extreme ordeals – bullying, rape, torture, incest, the extermination camps – but, on the other side of it, they bear the stigma of shame.

Survivors unsettle others; perhaps, in part, they upset the digestion of those who have not been through similar ordeals. But it is the survivors who feel the true shame.

Once again, the unsettlingly provocative Virginie Despentes puts her finger on this in her own ruggedly lyrical way: There is always something suspect about a girl who survives a rape, with people supposing that 'she liked it, then'.[1] Did she really put up a fight? Those who did not succumb under torture had to endure the same terrible suspicions, as Jean-Michel Chaumont recounts in his chilling investigation into Belgian communists tortured by the Gestapo.[2] How did they survive? *Given that they are still here*, can we really rule out the possibility that they talked to save their skins?

Primo Levi describes how the concentration camp survivors felt a curious shame after their liberation – a vague sensation that took the form of a gnawing anxiety or constant unease. In a chapter of *The Drowned and the Saved*,[3] he presents three facets of this feeling that will serve as anchors for our own discussion: shame after the event, the shame of 'why me?', and shame for the world.

The liberation of Auschwitz by Soviet troops on 27 January 1945 was not, in fact, a moment of great exultation for him. It marked the return of other preoccupations and anxieties: What had become of his nearest and dearest, and of society and politics in his native land? What had happened to all the people he knew? For months and sometimes years, the prisoners had lived without family or homeland. There was just their own body to look after and to protect from the cold, the hunger and the blows that rained down on them. A body that they had to keep going beyond the point of exhaustion as they desperately tried to stave off the moment of their planned, imminent and inevitable death. After their release, these men and women had to organise their return, re-engage with life and all its attendant worries, and feel once more the responsibilities of the world on their shoulders.

For Levi, shame after the event was prompted by recalling the living conditions in the camps. The Ancient Greeks distinguished between *zoe* and *bios*. *Bios* pertains to an existence structured by status, environment, life choices, tasks and plans. In other words, all the things that give shape to a life. *Zoe*, by contrast, pertains to the purely biological and cellular within us, to a structureless yet stubbornly persistent 'bare life'.[4] In the concentration camps, that is what life came down to: mustering up the strength not to die. The presence of the prefix *sur-* in survival is incongruous in that it does not connote an augmented quality (unlike Nietzsche's superman, Marx's surplus value or Foucault's surplus knowledge).[5] The survivor lives just enough not to die. At Auschwitz, surviving was the focus of every waking moment, necessitating a defensive and shabby selfishness. Showing respect, compassion and concern for one's neighbour becomes dangerous, writes Primo Levi. A moral code seems like a luxury that is not only useless but actively pernicious. Alain's provocative remark captures this idea with terrible succinctness: 'Morality is okay for the rich.'[6] The desperation not to die confiscates everything, inducing a lack of shame that is not based on contempt for others but the selfish drive to survive. The shame-based, socially regulated ethics we met earlier (*aidos*) applies to normal living, never to surviving. In contrast to those sinister cynics for whom the canons of shared morality are mere doormats on which to wipe their ambitions (for them, morality is okay for the poor), to the survivor it is seen as a dangerous luxury. After the event, Levi wonders: How could I have behaved like that, lacked such consideration for others and lived so like an animal, abandoning supposedly the most elementary rules of humanity? What have my persecutors turned me into? This is retrospective shame.

Among psychoanalysts, shame after the event assumes a precise clinical meaning associated with pain. A child who has been the victim of unfathomable sexual abuse early on may, at a later stage, when they arrive at puberty, ascribe a sexual meaning to the acts they once endured in moments of distress, stupefaction, solitude and incomprehension. They feel a delayed shame – an anxious malaise whose source they cannot pinpoint (unless they were to revisit the traumatic episodes).

This deferral points to the non-linearity of the psyche. It is really only phenomenologists, armed with a vertical awareness of their constituent forces, who are able to distinguish readily between retention ('I have memories of the past'), attention ('I focus on the present') and anticipation ('I have projects for the future'). The theory of the unconscious posits the idea of folds, loops and discontinuities in our psyche. There is no clear arrow of time that arranges experiences in sequential order, with the present progressively stacking up in the past and the future promising a fresh reserve of representations to one day add to the old.

The post-traumatic experience is expressed as a modal perfect: I *must have been* a victim of incest, I *must have been* raped. The event is not inscribed when it occurs; this process happens later on when I come to understand it and endow it with meaning by articulating it in a narrative. This delayed realisation can be captured in French by the use of the future perfect tense (a past that comes afterwards, a future that is inscribed beforehand).[7] This same tense is used to make promises: 'I promise I'll have finished this work by tomorrow.' I am speaking today as if tomorrow is already done, ascribing to an event to come the rock solidity of something in the past. It is also the tense of retrospective (and sometimes disenchanted) reckoning whereby anarchic ambitions and madcap desires are consigned to history: At the end of the day, I will only have achieved this or that. And it is also the tense of lucidity when we give ourselves up to God in prayer. Indeed, the tenses used in Christian prayer have been rather overlooked. In the present: 'Give us today our daily bread' (Help us welcome what is given to us.). In the past: 'Forgive us our trespasses' (Accept the mistakes already made.). In the future: 'Do not lead us into temptation' (Prevent any future straying from the path.). But these three requests all depend on the initial injunction of 'Thy will be done' being obeyed – in other words, regardless of what I do or say, things will ultimately end up having turned out just as He had decided in the first place. The future perfect tense is the echo of the Eternal in our temporal sensibilities.

∽

In a famous assertion, Lacan adopted it as the tense par excellence of the unconscious: It is what 'will have been',[8] which does rather suggest that God has been traded in for the unconscious ... To unpack this enigmatic formulation, we need to bear in mind that the unconscious is that which makes us ashamed. In Freud's earliest writings containing his first model of the psyche, shame is the central mechanism of repression: It is because they are shameful that desires are repressed and events forgotten. We have already met Phaedra,[9] the daughter of Minos and Pasiphaë and 'child of the light', who nevertheless in Racine's tragedy skulks in her residence, avoiding broad daylight because she is ashamed of her desires (in this case, her desperate love for her stepson). This is *not* guilt – we feel guilty about what we have done, but we are ashamed of our desires because they come across to us as monstrous or aberrant. They do not correspond to our values, convictions or accomplishments, and yet before we have even acted on our desires, they course through us, carry us away, escape our control and come to define us. Who am I that I can desire *that*?

It is worth recalling Freud's point that conscience is not merely an instrument for optimising our ability to adapt to external reality. It is forever engaged in the exhausting task of reining in our impossible desires and insane passions to prevent us from falling foul of social conventions and intransigent moral standards – it acts as a barrier to misplaced urges. We discussed earlier how narcissistic shame is the fallout of a painful relationship with reality. It is as if there is an impenetrable wall that thwarts our overweening ambitions, gives the lie to our supposed special abilities, and shatters our dreams of omnipotence.[10] But we can take this idea further. If *reality* is the name we give to that which resists us like a wall, perhaps we should accept that our true adversary is not so much the real as our insistent desires, ancient fears and deep-seated hang-ups. It is they that lead us to commit the same disastrous mistakes, to be drawn to the same types of people, and to suffer the same setbacks over and over.

The *reality* of our existence, and what makes us ashamed, is to be found in the midst of this commotion. For all our good intentions, bold resolutions and aspirations to greater self-discipline, what pops up around *every* corner is the unconscious: It is the implacable bane of our existence and dictator of our destiny. For all my bragging, grand declarations and stated ambitions, ultimately what I have *actually* achieved is this. And what will have thwarted me is not (just) bad luck, unfortunate encounters and missed opportunities, but the braking mechanisms within my own psyche. The unconscious in this sense is all that makes me ashamed – it introduces a disparity between what I believe I want and what *ultimately I really want*. We need only consider all our Freudian slips (which in fact convey a certain truth), all the anxieties that restrain us, and all our pathologically misplaced actions to appreciate that the unconscious is what writes our personal *history*.

What we call our past can be broken down into two streams of events: those that are conjugated in the past simple or present perfect and those that are conjugated in the future perfect. The past tenses (yesterday I did this, I ate that, I bumped into so-and-so) are used to describe anodyne, banal and dull events that initially leave a well-defined trace but are soon erased.

And then there is that which writes our history: those experiences that burst disruptively in on the present moment, piercing and tearing its fabric. An encounter, an emotion or something said or read disturbs me, provoking an inexplicable anxiety, an undefinable malaise. I feel impotent because I cannot grasp the meaning of what is happening to me, or else it resonates with past experiences that left enduring mental scars but were never put into words. These are the events whose meaning has been deferred, as if they have slipped below the radar (the sensors and transformers) of language, and just because they happened *before*, it does not mean they are *over*. Impossible secrets and secret wounds await a future mental configuration that will give expression to them and perhaps result in their resolution. There is a widespread belief that psychoanalysis comes down to saying that everything is the fruit of one's early years and that the past determines one's future. But the lesson it teaches us is exactly the opposite and hence more enigmatic: It is one's future that determines the past – a past that has not yet been *realised*.

Ultimately, the goal of psychoanalytic therapy is not to retrieve forgotten memories as if it were simply a question of teasing them out. It is to bring out those fragments of the past that until now have only existed as somatic blockages giving rise to repeated failures and incomprehensible behaviour. We certainly spend a lot of time trying to realise the future (accomplishing our dreams, keeping our promises, and so on), but what undermines these efforts is our failure to sufficiently 'realise the past'. To properly understand what this means, however, we need to make a distinction between the real and reality. The real is the event in its raw state – opaque, incomprehensible, dark and incomparable with anything else. And the real becomes reality when it is spoken, subjected to different interpretations and enmeshed in language. It only becomes reality long after it has occurred. Once again, we are in future perfect mode: The meaning of the past is supplied after the event.

Our early years are punctuated by stupefying discoveries, frightening ruptures, alarming emotions and unmanageable wounds. The English word *infant* and the French *enfant* ('child') both derive from the Latin *infans*, meaning speechless or inarticulate. They denote an individual who does not have enough language to keep the world at bay or to render it graspable, coherent or reasonable. Instead, the child is constantly subjected to unmediated incursions that they will only be able to articulate much later on.

To live is to conjugate the future perfect – the future imperfect? – of one's childhood.

After this somewhat lengthy detour, it is time to return to Primo Levi's shame after the event. It arises out of his alarming memories of concentration camp life when 'we had lived for months and years at an animal level'.[11] He asks himself how he could have accepted living like that, even if the animal reference is arguably an attempt to reassure himself. For the fact is that the survivors have not shed their humanity – rather, they have plumbed its depths. He is retrospectively stunned at the idea that he accepted this degraded state, at the total lack of shame and at the willingness to use every iniquitous and treacherous trick in the book to eat, drink, sleep and keep warm. Nothing was holding people back, and so they did not hold themselves back.

The situation was such, as Levi notes, that suicide was rare in Auschwitz. They did not have the time or energy, and 'there were other things to think about'.[12] The decision to commit suicide originates from an anguish in relation to a world and existence stripped of meaning, from a lack of prospects, and from a loss of dignity. In the case of the survivor, it is not as though they have found meaning and value in the simple fact of remaining alive. Their situation is such that they are beyond being able to articulate what meaning and value might even signify. In this diminished state, suicide is a luxury they can no longer afford.

❧

I indicated earlier that the survivor and the cynic, though they occupy opposing moral poles, both move beyond shame-based ethics, but we should also add the devoted parent and the ardent lover to that list. When we love someone that deeply, not even shame will hold us back; we are prepared to sacrifice our dignity and our own happiness if their health or well-being is at stake. I have in mind Verdi's *Rigoletto* (act II, scene III), when the buffoon casts off his sardonic and mocking persona in order to find out what has become of his daughter, whom he fears was kidnapped the day before. Soon enough, Rigoletto is bowing, prostrating himself and generally grovelling to the gentleman of the court – he has lost all shame and is humiliating himself. The change in the music is striking: We move from anger to lamentation, from harsh accusations (*Cortigiani, vil razza dannata* ...) to desperate pleas for pity (*Miei signori, perdono, pietate* ...). Rigoletto oversteps the bounds of decency for a jester, who should always retain his caustic wit. But he is no longer ashamed to beg, bootlick, weep and make a pathetic, humiliating spectacle of himself for his daughter's sake. The overcoming of his shame confirms the depth of his love. *Pietà, pietà, signori.* Shame no longer matters when it comes to those we love.

The second source of survivor's shame, writes Primo Levi, is summed up in that terrible question 'why me?' Though life was hanging by a thread, it did not break, and I am still here, whereas others better than I did not make it. The cast-iron rule in the camps seemed to be that it was the gentle, generous and loyal who died, while the cunning, selfish and cynical always found a way to hang on. Was it possible to survive the extermination camps for the 'right' reasons? Levi has the impression that he was simply very lucky, but can he really know that it was just down to luck? He wonders if every survivor has 'usurped his neighbour's place and lived in his stead. It is a supposition, but it gnaws at us'.[13]

As we have seen, shame is a question of how we are situated in relation to others, but, here, the concern is not whether one is in their rightful place; rather, it is the despairing feeling of having taken the place of someone else. Not least because a little inner voice is murmuring that it is simply the unwritten law of existence. It is always the bad ones who survive, somehow dodging the deadly bullets of life. Solidly ensconced, these heirs and beneficiaries of others' misfortune have always taken someone else's place, but a smokescreen of worthy words – merit, good fortune, talent, hard work – is erected to hide the shameful truth. Levi pierces the fog when he recalls Chjim, the watchmaker from Cracow, and Szabo, the taciturn Hungarian peasant.[14] The unbearable truth is that they – the good ones – are all dead.

In the face of the painfully blunt and anxiety-inducing question 'why me?', the very act of bearing witness as a survivor becomes problematic. The authentic witnesses, who experienced the ultimate truth of the violence, never came back. Their voice was definitively silenced. Some might object that the dignity and legitimacy of a witness derive from having been *present*, having seen it all with their own eyes and being in a position to speak in the first person. But, when it comes to the most extreme violence, only those who experienced the sheer horror of being gassed (before being burnt in the ovens), who died of sheer exhaustion, or who were beaten to death could really have spoken of it.

'I must repeat – we, the survivors, are not the true witnesses.'[15]

Levi agrees to speak from this position of indignity: I am here to bear witness to the fact that you do not come back alive from what I went through. It is an impossible and painful paradox, and once again the discrepancy gives rise to shame.

But why not talk about guilt here?[16] Would it not make more sense to talk of the survivor *feeling guilty* at not having died along with the others and interpreting their exceptional fate as a *moral fault* or a kind of betrayal? But, once again, it is a question of one's place in society: The survivor no longer feels that they are in their rightful place in the world of the living. When it comes to existence, they are superfluous to requirements, haunted by the idea that they should have died too. I feel out of place, or rather there is no longer any place for me here. The camps, where death was an industrial affair and the monotonous norm, have permanently assigned me another place, which is that of a corpse to be burnt.

The survivor may survive their losses – of innocence, ignorance, insouciance and trust in others – but they never quite feel that they have escaped once and for all. They feel they have no business living ordinary lives among other people and that they should have long ago joined the cohort of the dead. There is a suspended sentence hanging over them and they feel *out of step* in the world of the living. It is what Imre Kertész, who was deported to Auschwitz at the age of fourteen, called 'living the shame of life'.[17]

In the final chapter of *The Truce*, Primo Levi provides the key to the novel's title by recounting a recurring dream. He is sitting at his desk or else out walking, surrounded by family and friends. But suddenly he has the 'sensation of an impending threat' and everything – the scenery, the people – begins to collapse around him. As the anguish mounts, a realisation comes over him:

> I know what this thing means, and I also know that I have always known it; I am in the Lager once more, and nothing is true outside the Lager. All the rest was a brief pause, a deception of the senses, a dream; my family, nature in flower, my home.[18]

Finally, Primo Levi is no longer ashamed. Everything is becoming *normal* again as the nightmare recommences.

11

Intersectional Shame

Amid philosophical treatments of shame, the passage in Sartre's *Being and Nothingness* about the man who listens at doors stands out as essential reading. The aim is to analyse the genesis of self-consciousness through the gaze of the other, and Sartre argues that shame begins with the feeling of being seen, watched, caught out and objectified. In my own company, I feel no shame and indulge in coarse behaviour, dressing in a slovenly way, snorting loudly and stuffing my face with food. But in the company of others, everything changes: 'My original fall is the existence of the Other.'[1]

The scene unfolds as follows. I walk down the stairs in my apartment block, floor by floor, until at one point the temptation becomes too strong. I stop and listen at one of the doors and look through the keyhole. Am I motivated by jealousy, vice or curiosity? Will I catch snatches of conversation or am I hoping to make out a silhouette?

During all this time, with my senses on the alert, I am no more than the consciousness of the fascinating spectacle on the other side of the door. 'But all of a sudden I hear footsteps in the hall. Someone is looking at me!'[2] I give a start and my whole body begins shaking. I feel anxiety, embarrassment and shame: What on earth are they going to think of me?

And, suddenly, the 'self' erupts – is precipitated – into existence by the Other. It is the presence of another, even if it is only *assumed*, that makes me myself exist. It is that version of the self that exists in the gaze of others and is fixed in place by their judgements (though can we meaningfully call the other version – that turmoil of dreams and shifting emotions – the self?). It is all over for the eye (the pure consciousness) at the keyhole – I have become characterised as *someone who is* perverted, jealous or immoral. The neighbours' chins are wagging, and I no longer belong to myself. Before all this, I was nothing but a consciousness intensely focused on some kind of spectacle behind a door, and, suddenly, I have become the voyeur of the building. I am ashamed, therefore I am.

This analysis by Sartre captures something essential. He is not interested in how shame comes into being but, rather, how shame makes *us* come into being. There is, of course, the initial birth, which no one can be aware of: that initial trauma of a little body being plucked from the womb whose only tangible trace for us is a date on our passport and the tender tales told by our parents. The true birth happens later. When Sartre talks of the 'original fall', he means becoming rigidly defined by particular events and having superficial labels attached to oneself. I only become aware of my 'self' beneath the gaze of the Other, who traps me in a stereotyped version thereof.

What Sartre describes in terms of a fundamental ontology has been recast in more personally painful terms by intersectional studies and countless first-person accounts from women, blue-collar workers and racial minorities. In these narratives, the self is not so much objectified as *reduced* (to clichés, pure functionality, and so on), *alienated* by being designated as irremediably inferior, *discriminated against* and consigned to the margins, and *stigmatised* and excluded for departing too far from the social norm (disability, alcohol, etc.). Frantz Fanon in *Black Skin, White Masks*, Simone Weil in *Journal d'usine* (about her year spent working in a factory), and Annie Ernaux in *A Woman's Story* and *A Man's Place* bring Sartre into the everyday world, giving substance to his analysis and extending it.

We shift from the young man caught listening at doors in a Haussmann apartment building to the daily humiliations and insulting marginalisation of ethnic minorities, women and the working class, all perpetuated by the dominant institutions and systems.

This highlights a point that I did not address earlier when discussing social contempt – shame, I argued, did not automatically follow from humiliation but required an internalisation of the social gaze (and an implicit endorsement of oppressive norms). I did indicate that social contempt insidiously tends to lead to self-denigration, with a poor person, for example, ending up believing they are responsible for their own circumstances (for want of ambition, out of laziness, and so on). By the same token, a phallocratic system tends to turn a victim into the guilty party: A woman who has been sexually assaulted and then constantly socially demeaned ends up believing that she somehow provoked or at least permitted the assault, or else that she should be satisfied with whatever redress a misogynist system deigns to accord her.

But I did not consider the concrete contexts in which shame is generated, such as the atmosphere in a factory supervised by a sadistic foreman, or in an office run by a petty-minded line manager, or at school. And then there are the mechanisms of selection and discrimination, and the colonial systems. By repeatedly and insistently humiliating and belittling people, these situations systematically manufacture a shame that is difficult to shake off, for it ends up underpinning and structuring our own self-image. These shame-generating frameworks have three central features that I will briefly address in turn (though each would merit a whole book to itself).

The first is a process of inferiorisation perpetuated by the uneven distribution of power and wealth, by public institutions such as schools or the judiciary, and by pseudo-science that posits a hierarchy of race, gender and class and justifies the supercilious and infantilising gaze of the dominant class. This incessant demeaning of people provokes an unspoken, simmering rage, which is captured with unique intensity in the novels of Richard Wright, and a terrible inability to express it, for fear of harsh and immediate retribution.[3] The derogatory and dismissive remarks rain down unrelentingly, contemptuous looks, micro-aggressions and snap judgements become our daily lot, and the constant assault ends up enclosing our soul in a carapace. It is henceforward trapped between the grey moroseness of shame and explosions of anger in reaction to that shame.

In a fine collection of interviews, Pierre Bergounioux has shown how the French state education system (he spent decades teaching French literature in secondary schools in disadvantaged suburbs), despite its stated goals, is in fact a machine for deepening the sense of indignity felt by the most vulnerable. 'Children starting secondary school at the age of eleven who are not well versed in state school values and practices will be reminded of their shortcomings and mediocrity several times a day.'[4]

Passive acceptance lies at the end of that particular road. The dominated are afforded as little scope for initiative as possible, and women are kept out of decision-making posts – they are made to submissively execute instructions and nothing more. Female blue-collar workers are always the most expendable cog in the machine, while their white-collar sisters are simple pawns who will be sacrificed soon enough – they are nothings in the general scheme of things.

Marx explains in *Capital* how industrial capitalism tends to transform everything, including workers, into a commodity: My labour power becomes something that I sell to the highest bidder rather than being a source of moral worth. Once that stage is reached, everything becomes tradeable for profit. Financial capitalism takes things even further by promoting the notion of expendability: There is no longer any need to exploit workers to make a profit since one can simply sack them and automatically increase the company's share price. I am reminded of the female factory workers at Daewoo in François Bon's story, who were cynically exploited for the shareholders' benefit as if they were worth nothing more than the metal shavings, leftover waste and other detritus all around them.[5] People are ashamed of being treated like an object or commodity to be exploited, then as junk (a wreck ready for the scrapyard), and finally as nothing at all. The manager and decision-maker enters a room where a meeting is due to be held and where the cleaner is still going about her business. He curses: '*Nobody's* bloody here yet ...' The simple but compelling lesson that Simone Weil took away from her proletarian immersion (operating a cutting machine at Alstom and a milling machine at Renault) was this:

Human beings are divided into two categories: the people who count for something and the people who count for nothing. When you're in the

second, you end up finding it normal that you count for nothing –
which isn't to say that you don't suffer.[6]

The second mechanism involves reducing people to stereotypes. It is not exactly inferiorisation but rather assigning
shorthand, unremovable labels to others. In the social sciences,
this reduction to clichés goes by the name of *essentialism* or *natu-
ralism*. James Baldwin writes of this:

> I was ashamed of where I'd come from and where I'd been and
> ashamed of the life in the church and ashamed of my father.
> Ashamed of the blues and ashamed of jazz and, of course, ashamed
> of watermelon because it was, you know, all of these stereotypes
> that the country inflicts on Negroes.[7]

This kind of reduction is unwittingly reinforced by the well-
meaning anti-racist who declares their love of jazz when meeting
an African American or extols the merits of Zen Buddhism in the
presence of Asians. Before they have even opened their mouth,
somebody from an ethnic minority is rigidly pigeonholed according to their supposed tastes or lifestyle. And to top it all, they
are expected to be grateful to the exoticism-loving 'native' from
the majority ethnicity for their interest in different cultures, as if
simply inverting the value attached to clichés will sort the problem
of racism. But it is the clichés themselves that humiliate and per-
emptorily curtail the range of possibilities open to an individual.
A woman can only love her children and her home; a blue-collar
worker is necessarily irresponsible and devoid of ambition. In
his study of the Cockerill factories, Cédric Lomba shows what
a dim and stereotyped opinion the company's executives have
of the workers, whom they see as stuck in the past ('They resist

any change') and as slackers ('They down tools on the slightest pretext').[8] The primary function of cliché is to shield ourselves from other people's humanity. We prefer to hide behind stereotypes because they serve as an alibi for reprehensible behaviour: If they are lazy, we are not exploiting them, and if they are inferior anyway, how can we be debasing them?

The third mechanism is stigmatisation. Rather than superimposing a cliché dreamt up in the neurotic minds of the dominant class, this involves picking up on the slightest difference and turning it into a means to denigrate and exclude the possessor of that trait. It need not be much: a downward glance to judge the quality of a jacket, a slight smile on hearing a hint of an accent or spelling out one's words when talking to someone. All these things *create a distance* and make the other person feel as if they have been *found out*, even though they were not trying to hide anything. Whether the dominant individual is exaggerating their empathy (no, I am not a racist; yes, I really like the company of poor people, and so on) or frankly expressing their contempt, the result is the same: I am made to feel that I stick out like a sore thumb, which is to say I feel both terribly conspicuous and completely out of place. And the combination of the two gives rise to shame.

Stigmatisation need not involve deep humiliation – a question dripping with condescending kindness will do the trick: 'And so where are you from?' It is worth reading the converging accounts of three women on this point: Christiane Taubira, Isabelle Boni-Claverie, and Tania de Montaigne.[9] For the person *asking* the question, the meaning is this: 'Look at me, I am not racist; the fact that I am showing such an interest in the exotic roots of another person proves just how open-minded I am.' And when the answer comes – ordinary French regions like Val-d'Oise, Auvergne or some such – the invariable follow-up is: 'No, I mean where are you from *originally*?' It is this type of remark that makes the other person feel out of place and marginalised – they are only allowed to occupy the place that I allocate to them. One might object that I am exaggerating, or else that these are just faux pas or atavistic reflexes that are gradually going extinct in this casteless age that is so much more 'tolerant' and accepting of diversity. But what is so terrible about tolerance, as the name implies, is the hesitating acceptance it implies: the apparent yes that may conceal a no. The true antithesis of tolerance is love …

The other point to bear in mind is made by Marx in a different context. In *On the Jewish Question*, he argues that just because a state no longer officially recognises any religion, this does not mean that faith has died out. The end of state religions tends in fact to be associated with a diversification of the religious urge. Whether this takes the shape of watered-down beliefs, convoluted doctrines or community-based faiths, there is still some kind of afterlife, personal transcendence and potential for keeping people in thrall. Only a 'social transformation' would signal the end of religions, in Marx's view. In the same way (*mutatis mutandis*, of course), the abolition of slavery, the end of colonial empires and the repealing of racist laws never meant the end of racism or its gradual suppression but a shift to something more nebulous. The terrible, recurring and very public humiliations that used to happen completely legally have given way to a more insidious era of ill-defined shame, provoked by a pursing of the lips, a frown, a change of tone depending on who is being addressed, and more seriously by the hypocrisy of systems of selection and evaluation.

These three assaults on the person ('you're nothing', 'you're a cliché', 'you're out of place here') result in shame being a constant and relentless dimension of one's existence, whether it be the distress occasioned by a critical gaze (those cruel moments of public embarrassment when you want the ground to swallow you up) or the uncomfortable self-generated experience (*aidos*) that is designed to ward off shame. Intersectional shame is a state of consciousness and a condition of existence that alienates me from myself, penetrating more deeply than lifestyle questions or my relationships with others. I end up being able to relate to myself only through the sickly prism of shame: I constantly feel worthless, invariably a cliché and always out of place.

The brilliance of Fanon, Baldwin and W. E. B. Du Bois was to identify how racism shapes one's perception of oneself: I realise that I am black beneath the white gaze, writes Fanon in 'The Lived Experience of the Black Man'.[10] Before, I was just a man or woman determined to make the most of life. But, then, I realise that this body that keeps me alive and is the vehicle of my interaction with the world causes a problem for a certain class of person, which happens to be the dominant class with all the power and privileges. White people do not perceive me on the standard wavelength (ranging from well-disposed to neutral). Even if it is only fleetingly, they stare at me as if I am a problem ('Being a problem is a strange experience.').[11]

But though black people may be an invention of white people, the converse is not true, as Baldwin points out. There's no reversibility or reciprocity because 'White is a metaphor for power, and that is simply a way of describing Chase Manhattan Bank.'[12]

Instead, there's what Baldwin calls 'this cloud that stood between them [his fellow black people] and the sun, between them and love and life and power, between them and whatever it was that they wanted', an obstacle and barrier that is one's own self as projected by the wild imaginings of the dominant class.[13]

A woman comes to construe herself as black (which is to say simultaneously different and inferior) in a white imagination (that is also male and bourgeois) that has taken possession of her soul like an army of occupation. Shame is the state of being able to conceive of oneself only within the constraints (on one's aspirations or abilities) imposed by another. The obstacles erected to my dignity, the barriers to my dreams and the restrictions on my potential become hardwired into me, alienating me from myself, holding me back and ultimately defining me. I am hampered by my own self, but a self that is the product of the painful splinter that others have planted within me.

> Shame. Shame and self-contempt. Nausea. When they like me, they tell me my color has nothing to do with it. When they hate me, they add that it's not because of my color. Either way, I am a prisoner of the vicious circle.[14]

12
Systemic Shame

To return to Primo Levi, the third and final type of shame he identifies is 'being ashamed of being a man',[1] or as he puts it elsewhere: 'And there is another, vaster shame, the shame of the world.'[2]

After all, this world that is all adrift is also mine. I am part of it and I cannot pretend to a neutrality that would isolate me from it to the point of becoming insensitive to it. John Donne's 1624 'Meditation XVII' is germane here:

No man is an island, entire of itself; every man is a piece of the continent, a part of the main [...] any man's death diminishes me, because I am involved in mankind, and therefore never send to know for whom the bell tolls; it tolls for thee.

This is the principle of solidarity. It is not that I should feel guilty for the iniquities of the world, but I cannot help but be affected and sullied by them. The marker of the shame of the world is a double negative: I cannot not be affected, and this is what introduces the feeling of pain and bitterness. Being ashamed of the world is not to actively acknowledge one's complicity or to declare one's absolute determination to change things. It is more a case of not being able to resist the feeling of being implicated in this sorry state of affairs.

Being ashamed of being a man is also how Levi characterises his feelings after leaving the concentration camp, a phrase picked up by Deleuze who adds: 'There's no better reason for writing.'[3] Shame is the wellspring par excellence of thinking, creating, writing and doing philosophy. Over twenty centuries after Plato, Deleuze puts shame back at the centre of philosophical thought. But what does 'being ashamed of being a man' mean exactly? It no doubt has to do for a start with belonging to an animal species which has had such a desperately sad and regrettable track record over the one hundred or so centuries since the Neolithic Revolution. That species has turned our shared home into one gigantic rubbish dump, pillaging and trashing everything. Its seemingly limitless capacity for inflicting pain and suffering is so disturbing that perhaps the only consolation available to us is that articulated by Lévi-Strauss in *Tristes Tropiques*: 'The world began without man and will end without him.'[4] The human race corresponds to a difficult period that the world just has to get through.

This, then, is the first layer of meaning: I belong to the same species as the torturers, persecutors and criminals. They are my fellow human beings and there is little reason to be proud of my human family. 'And then, finally, we also felt a certain shared, human responsibility, for the fact that Auschwitz was the work of humankind and we are humans. It is a product of the civilization we live in.'[5]

But when Deleuze goes on to say that this shame prompts him to write, think and create, we might ask what it contains in the way of a creative spark. What we need to bear in mind is that 'humankind' in this context refers to all that is most base (and basic) within us: spinelessness, cowardice, selfishness, vileness, avarice, treachery and the like. I have in mind the characters in Céline's works or the lawyer Derville at the end of Balzac's novella *Colonel Chabert*. The titular colonel is a hero of the Napoleonic Wars who is wrongly declared dead and then forgotten, stripped of his possessions, ruined and rejected by his 'widow', who owes her fortune to him. The loyal Derville attempts to defend his interests but fails and, disgusted by humankind, he resolves to withdraw from society, as far away from his fellow human beings as possible. *Deep down*, human beings are a crucible of vile and ignominious passions that boil over time and again behind the closed doors of Derville's office when inheritances have to be divvied up. That is when the masks come off, any pretence of generosity vanishes, and mutual respect, fraternity and love fizzle out entirely. Shame is a sort of resistance mechanism in the face of humanity at its most base. We recoil and detach ourselves in disgust; we flee this grotesque caricature of humanity, unceasingly abject and vile. And we fear falling prey to the same petty-mindedness and being caught up in the whirl of moral turpitude, so powerfully does it seem to be sucking us in. Hence the desire to open ourselves up to other futures, which Deleuze describes as 'animal' possibilities, by which he simply means different and instinctual possibilities.

Art is a reaction to this shame in that it appeals to the unbounded and the expansive, hinting at potential routes to the elsewhere:

> What seems to me the highest and the most difficult achievement of Art is not to make us laugh or cry, or to rouse our lust or our anger, but to do as nature does – that is, fill us with wonderment.[6]

Philosophy also engages in this effort to shift our frame of reference, to see things from other perspectives and to expand our horizons. As we saw when discussing Lacan, its function is to resist the asinine thanks to the shame associated with it. And by the asinine, we mean facile, narrow, second-hand and mechanical thinking, dull certainties and socially in-vogue attitudes (we certainly do *not* mean thinking that comes from less privileged and educated quarters, without all the standard trappings of academia). All important concepts in philosophy involve an expansion of the mind. By engaging with them, we rise above that base crucible of humanity and open ourselves up to other perspectives and different life trajectories – we open ourselves up to thinking like an octopus, perceiving the world like a tick and feeling it like a jaguar.

Art and philosophy expose us to being ashamed of ourselves, not in the form of a morose guilt or a despairing affliction but as a stimulus to striking out across pastures new.

The general shame of belonging to the human race assumes a more specific focus through the relationships we entertain with the history of our people, nation and even family. This attachment can be a painful experience: I am part of a national community that shapes my identity, having been born in a country that I have grown to love, but now corrupt and cynical political leaders are implementing iniquitous policies, leading us into impossible wars and ruthlessly repressing dissent, and I am ashamed of it all. After the terrible days of 1848 when 4,000 insurgents demonstrating against the closing of the National Workshops were killed, George Sand wrote: 'What days of tears and indignation these have been! I am ashamed of being a Frenchwoman today, I who used to be so proud of it.'[7]

A century later another woman, stunned when she found out about French colonial policies, declared:

I will never forget the moment when I felt and understood, for the first time, the tragedy of colonization.

[...] Since that day, I have been ashamed of my country. Since that day, I cannot meet an Indochinese person, an Algerian, a Moroccan, without wanting to ask his forgiveness. Forgiveness for all the pain, all the humiliations that he has been subjected to, that his people have been subjected to. For their oppressor is the French State, which acts in the name of all French people, and therefore also, to a small degree, in my own name. That is why, in the presence of those whom the French state oppresses, I cannot but blush.[8]

It is patriotic shame full of rage towards unworthy political leaders and incompetent military commanders leading the country into disaster; it is shame imbued with indignation at the injustice of it all; but there is also a sense of a love betrayed, of battered pride. As Carlo Ginzburg puts it: 'The country we call ours is the one that we are capable of feeling ashamed of.'[9]

Patriotic shame is, above all, the expression of the anger of the governed towards their so-called representatives. But there is one final type of shame that is more specific still and pertains to a painful relationship with one's personal lineage. J. M. Coetzee, who was born into a family of Afrikaner colonisers and witnessed the introduction of apartheid when he was eight years old, found himself wondering about the dynasty of persecutors from which he originated: How many generations of oppressors have led up to me? It is not membership of the human race that is at issue here, or even of a specific national community, but the objective bond I have – the blood ties and shared cultural heritage – with the tyrant caste, the dominant elite. In his novels up to and including *Disgrace*, Coetzee explores the shame of the heir to privilege and member of the oppressor class, which automatically denatures and complicates one's dealings with others. Even when I am just saying hello to a person of colour, I cannot help intimating my apologies, to the point where it becomes embarrassing and almost humiliating – the result is, after all, to insist on a person's origins (shame is sometimes little better than contempt in its effects). But this shame also tempers my love for my family and friends since there is this unspoken loathing for what they are and what they represent.

This *systemic* shame – that is, the shame associated with being part of the dominant Establishment – cares nothing for my personal life choices or the values I defend. It is the shame of the heir to privilege and social dominance. But even alluding to it tends to get people's backs up and make them feel uncomfortable. As soon as one raises the notion of systemic racism, systemic gender inequality or systemic stigmatisation, there is a defensive reaction which is especially noticeable among the spoilt (and sensitive) children of the baby boomers.

Their incredulous reaction tends to be: 'Why on earth should I be ashamed, with my altruistic beliefs, my attachment to human rights and universal values, and my visceral aversion to all forms of oppression and political extremism? I have always respected my fellow human beings, fought discrimination, demanded greater social justice, defended women's rights and condemned racism. And as for being privileged ... Look how much I am earning after years of studying, and compare that to what the fat cats are getting. I think you have picked the wrong target.'

Behind these indignant protestations, one can sense discomfort and fear. The fear is that if I *do* have reason to be ashamed, then clearly something is wrong that needs to be put right. But protest requires energy, and the current system has after all served me rather well ... The discomfort lies in having to jettison my tranquil conscience and the smile I wake up with in the morning when I consider my successful life – when I reflect on having an apartment big enough to be able to invite friends over to talk about the scandalous plight of migrants. The only concession you will hear from these people is the earnest acknowledgement that they have been very lucky and are conscious of having led privileged lives. At the same time, do not forget their personal merit. 'I've been lucky.' Perhaps, but your luck has come at a cost for others. 'You've no idea how hard I've had to work, I've earned everything by the sweat of my brow!' Except that these days, if you do not have any connections or capital behind you, success is likely to elude you no matter how hard you try – the only 'merit' of many people is to have been born at the right time in the right place.

Merit and luck? *But to what extent can I claim that all the things I possess have not always in a sense been taken from someone else?* Take the white, educated middle-class man in good health with a permanent job who owns his own house, is comfortably off, orders takeaways (with a tip, of course, for the delivery man) and is nice to his cleaning lady. That guy is not ashamed, he does not *want* to be ashamed or allow his clear conscience to be ruffled. And the coup de grâce – the final hypocrisy – is that he will attempt to justify himself: 'I would frankly be ashamed to feel ashamed – it would be perverse. The shame that really needs to be addressed is that of the poor, of ethnic minorities, of women …' That is all very well, but the point is that we also need to question our own role in the shame that they have experienced. Objections are to be expected from the other direction too: 'Now wait a minute, the whole point is that we are made to feel *too* ashamed the whole time. We are fed up with all this futile virtue signalling and pointless beating up of ourselves – we need to adopt a more relaxed attitude towards our heritage and cultural reflexes.'

But this is also to completely miss the point, since it is impossible to be 'too ashamed'. Some people may well make a song and dance about their purported feelings of guilt to lend themselves a certain gravitas, but this does not happen with shame. They do not want to feel the repressed anger that would come with shame and would prevent them speaking with such fluency and rhetorical grace of the disinherited, the vulnerable and the migrants.

Shame ought to be the price to pay – the minimum in union dues that they should be expected to cough up – for the person born into privilege whose history is marked by slavery, genocides, colonial empires, discrimination against women and the exploitation of the most vulnerable. You can be sure that the vulnerable and dominated will have paid a more exorbitant price. And, in answer to the Sunday Spinozists and erstwhile Nietzscheans – who see this fixation with suffering as negative and replete with resentment – we should turn once again to Primo Levi. The shame of the world has a precise function, he reminds us, which may be limited but can be decisive: It serves to immunise us.[10] It can potentially prevent a repetition of the horror and a return of the hatred. Though Levi cannot help but ask: How long will the antibodies remain effective for?

Those who refuse to entertain the idea of this kind of shame are the same ones who denounce quotas under the banner of gender-blind universalism during sterile parliamentary debates. It used to be the case that I was excluded from a particular post or status because I was a woman or from an ethnic minority or from a disadvantaged background. And now people are complaining that I only stand a chance of obtaining them because of my social background, my skin colour or my gender! It seems they win either way, though not necessarily when it comes to self-awareness, as Baldwin acidly points out.

Shame in the form of intersectional suffering – the shame of being 'on the wrong side of the tracks' – forces one to reflect on the mechanisms of injustice, detect hypocrisy, anticipate danger and play a calculating game. You have never really had to look at me, writes Baldwin, but I have had no choice but to observe you carefully to avoid trouble and gain some perspective on my suffering. I know more about you than you do about me because the dominated are obliged to doubt and call themselves into question. And to realise that, although society would have them believe otherwise, their failures cannot exclusively be down to themselves. In analysing the way white people behave towards black people in America, men towards women, and the exploiters towards the exploited, Baldwin concludes that they continuously lie to themselves, distort reality and kid themselves about their merits. The eternal victors lap up heroic myths about their families and their country to obscure their own monstrous reflection in the mirror. They are so saturated with lies that they become 'innocent', in the sense that they are sincerely ignorant of the criminality of their acts. They simply do not see the suffering they are causing. Whether it be in terms of their career, marriage, wealth or social standing, they find constant confirmation that their success *is* based on their own merits.

> They have destroyed and are destroying hundreds of thousands of lives and do not know it and do not want to know it ... But it is not permissible that the authors of devastation should also be innocent. It is the innocence which constitutes the crime.[11]

The opposite of innocence is not guilt but lucidity – ultimately, that was the lesson of Genesis all that time ago. And someone who is ashamed is lucid: They can see the injustices and iniquities sanctioned by the law, the courts and the Church.

To what extent might we assert that shame – that fretful frame of mind that is highly alert to signs and signals – overlaps with intelligence? In *Notes from Underground*, Dostoevsky paints the portrait of a depressive fortysomething with a kidney disease who refuses to get treatment for it, preferring instead to make the most of the money he has recently inherited.[12] This retired civil servant goes to extraordinary lengths to create situations where he will be belittled and exposed to ridicule. It is as if he is getting a perverse pleasure out of being humiliated.

It would be easy enough to diagnose some form of mental pathology and write him off as a masochist, but Dostoevsky is not painting the portrait of a pervert. Rather, he is elucidating what it is to be ashamed and the form in which it is most commonly experienced, namely as conscience. We have already evoked conscience as a sort of moral arbiter (the superego) when talking about narcissistic shame. But here it is a case of something even more elementary: conscience as a gap or discrepancy. Conscience defers and plays for time, putting the brakes on our instinctive reflexes and interrupting the flow: 'So what should I do now? Think for a moment. Take your time. Ask yourself the question.' These intervals, these temporary lulls, these fleeting shadows are conscience at work.

The antihero of *Notes from Underground* is fascinated by what he calls 'men of action', which is to say those who exist in a world of immediacy where there is no distinction between thought and action. When they drink or fight, they do so wholeheartedly and unreflectingly, without losing any sleep over it. They fully inhabit their characters, whether it be in the role of loyal friend, valiant soldier or life and soul of the party – they are life's shameless ones. They throw themselves into everything without second thoughts and with a completely clear conscience. They are what Baldwin would call the 'innocent'.

By contrast, the narrator of *Notes from Underground* is a sucker for conscience. The wound to the psyche that it constitutes and the negativity that it generates overshadow everything. It is like a second layer draped over reality that introduces perpetual hesitation. Conscience prompts us to rehash everything and rake over the ashes of the past (I should have done this, said that, and so on), trapping us in feelings of resentment. It serves to shatter the myth of reality: Watching a friend having a good time, a boss losing his temper or a wife doing her hair yet again, I find myself wondering, but what are these roles they are playing, how can they not be brought up short by their own vanity? Conscience reveals everything to be a comedy of masks and at the same time undermines conventional moral oppositions. It sets off a vibration that fractures fixed identities. Why, for example, would we not find accomplished models of humankind among drunks, prostitutes or losers rather than among all those 'functioning' types?

A clear conscience is not a conscience in this sense but a self-satisfied rut. Conscience oozes a negativity that fractures the external world, an acid that eats away at the beautiful masks. Shame is accompanied by reserves of lucidity that may be despairing but are also immense.

13

Revolutionary Shame

In Rostand's play, there is the famous reply of Cyrano to the young fool who tries to humiliate him by drawing attention to his huge, misshapen nose (a 'disability' that others rarely dare mention for fear of provoking his terrible ire). The upstart steps forward and declares: 'Monsieur, you have a nose that is ...' And then pauses for inspiration, which unfortunately for him is not forthcoming: 'very big'. Whereupon Cyrano pretends to be offended ('Monsieur, you can surely do better') and reels off in front of everyone, in poetic and baroque fashion, all the witticisms and nasty remarks that his protuberance has prompted over the years. It is a magical tirade. Cyrano's case is admittedly ambiguous because he no doubt suffers from this salient characteristic that cloaks him in ugliness, or so he feels. But in this act of poetic revenge ('A cape, no! A peninsular!'), Cyrano indicates one strategy for turning things around.

There is a marked tendency in the present age to reflect shame back, as evidenced in the slogans cited in the introduction, such as 'The shame is yours, not ours' or 'Stop being ashamed of who you are.' There are various strategies for turning things around, which we could group together under four headings: inversion, projection, subversion and purification.

The inversion that Cyrano pointed the way towards is reminiscent of the Nietzschean project of 're-evaluating all values'. This involves being proud of something that one might have been secretly ashamed of, of publicly and wholeheartedly embracing something that was shamefully kept from view or was the source of an inferiority complex. Perhaps the best-known example, and rightly so, is Gay Pride, which is all about embracing – with pride, impertinence and exultation – a sexuality that was once condemned as deviant. One asserts one's sexual difference but at the same time one's happy affiliation to an ethos, to a way of being and constructing one's identity, and to a community. A similar logic applies to physical discrimination. In a world obsessed with slim and trim bodies, the overweight and generous-bellied have fought back, embracing their figures and seeing their bodies not as a source of shame but a positive marker of difference that can be related to questions of identity and culture, as well as conceptualised (witness the development of fat studies).

And, to resume our earlier discussion of discrimination on the basis of skin colour, one can also to some extent assimilate the concept of *négritude* developed and promoted by Aimé Césaire and Léopold Senghor to this strategy of inversion, since it involves embracing a cultural heritage, rooting oneself in a rich identity and proclaiming one's affiliation to a community of values. The greatest poets, in collections bearing appropriately eloquent titles (*Hosties noires*,[1] *Minerai noir*[2]) celebrate blackness as perfection, as colour in all its plenitude, as an inextinguishable radiance of dizzying depths. Inversion is an elementary tactic that is effective in its very simplicity: not only accepting something within oneself but publicly asserting one's difference. Negative judgements and stigmas are dismantled and done away with through an inner conversion which is then shared in forthright fashion with the external world. There is a pride in being oneself.

The second way of turning things round in one's favour takes the form of a projection, or more precisely of displacing the shame. This again is captured in the slogan we've already seen ('The shame is yours, not ours'), which is often brandished against rapists and perpetrators of incest and other sexual assaults at the moment of unmasking them – in other words, all those whose impunity derived from the shame felt by their victims. As we saw earlier, Ferenczi revealed the mechanism for the initial displacement: Sexual abusers offload the burden of shame associated with their act onto a victim who is incapable of filtering or neutralising it because their state of shock has rendered them permeable to the emotions of the perpetrator, which they will feel as if those emotions were their own.[3] And so, it is a case of 'return to sender', though this transfer is at the same time a transmutation. In being transferred back, this shame changes nature: It is no longer the anxiety associated with something unnameable that is happening to me but the public proclamation of an ignominy that belongs to the perpetrator.

The third strategy is subversion. We have already mentioned the Cynics, the Franciscans and Gandhi in our discussion of social contempt. Each, in their own way, made a point of occupying the social space assigned to them by those who held them in contempt, and in so doing made a virtue out of it and an implicit criticism. Gandhi always travelled third-class in a handwoven cotton dhoti; the Cynics' worldly possessions amounted to a cloak (that served as both coat and roof over their head), a staff and a leather pouch; the Franciscans had their vow of poverty. But it would be a misconception to see in this austerity simply a classic rejection of material wealth in favour of inner richness. It is more a case of occupying poverty as a space of ordeals, fortifying humiliations and opportunities for exercising one's capacities. Actively electing radical poverty is a provocation that rests not on preaching and speechifying but on a direct demonstration and visible adoption of a way of life.

Jean Genet further ramps up the power of such provocations by adding other dimensions and occupying other spaces of 'infamy', namely destitution (that space beyond poverty), homosexuality and delinquency.[4] I am thinking of the challenge that Genet set himself after the idea came to him in the depths of opprobrium at the Mettray penal colony, where young delinquents were sent to be 'rehabilitated' and 'disciplined'. In *The Thief's Journal*, he writes: 'I felt the cruel shame of having my head shaved, of being dressed in unspeakable clothes, of being confined in that vile place.'[5]

How am I supposed to 'weather my desolation'? he asks himself. The answer he finds is to submit himself to a rigorous discipline that he likens to a spiritual exercise, a particular ethical method of his own: 'The mechanism was somewhat as follows (I have used it since): to every charge brought against me, unjust though it be, from the bottom of my heart I shall answer yes.'[6]

It is not about erasing the shame or converting it into a source of pride but, rather, latching on to the humiliation and using it as a tool. It is about occupying the space created by the insult ('I owned up to being the coward, traitor, thief and fairy they saw in me') and reappropriating it for oneself.[7] This should emphatically not be confused with a process of interiorisation – an acceptance of the legitimacy of the insult – that leads to a painful sense of resignation and self-contempt. Rather, it is a vigorous introjection set as a challenge to oneself and others: Yes, I will be the 'coward,

traitor, thief and fairy', but I will be those things to excess, more
wildly than you ever dared imagine in your stigmatising fantasies.
This is not exactly an alchemical transformation of shame into
pride but a *free and willing* descent into shame and opprobrium.
Genet takes the 'vile place' he has been confined to and turns it
into a garden of delights, a space for creation and pleasure and a
mellifluous soundbox. In rejecting me, you have freed me from
the constraints of banality and mediocrity.

After two years of sticking scrupulously to this new discipline,
he notes that 'I was strong' and that 'I became abject'.[8] The poeti-
cally embraced abjection ends up troubling the stigmatising party
and undermining their efforts to reject and exclude. I very much
want to conduct my purge and cast you out, they say, but only if
I can secretly continue to control your fall from grace and constantly use it to affirm my own superiority. In becoming abject,
the humiliated party averts the intended condemnation – they turn
their rejection into a transgression and a source of pleasure that
fascinates in return. It is then the tormentors who find themselves
locked into a certain attitude and forced to confront certain truths
about themselves as reflected in the abject state of the other. They
become a prisoner of their own hypocrisy, whereas the stigmatised
party revels in their shame and finds a form of freedom from this
strange, shifted perspective.

'"At least," I said to myself, "if my shame is real, it hides a
sharper, more dangerous element, a kind of sting that will always
threaten anyone who provokes it."'[9]

The fourth approach is through purification. This involves giving
expression to the element of pure anger that shame contains.

Primo Levi's description of the liberation of Auschwitz in *The
Truce* will serve to illustrate the point. The Germans have deserted

the camp shortly before the arrival of the Soviet troops and four young Russian soldiers approach on horseback. They discover the battered huts, the corpses sprawled everywhere and finally the haggard, skeletal survivors with their thousand-yard stares. What Levi sees in their eyes is not only the expected pity and compassion but also an oppressive and less expected awkwardness and embarrassment that seals their lips. What he recognises in their eyes is shame:

> It was that shame we knew so well, the shame that drowned us after the selections, and every time we had to watch, or submit to, some outrage: the shame the Germans did not know, that the just man experiences at another man's crime; the feeling of guilt that such a crime should exist, that it should have been introduced irrevocably into the world of things that exist, and that his will for good should have proved too weak or null, and should not have availed in defence.[10]

The shame of the just arises when they become painfully aware of their impotence at the sight of such human degradation. This is quite distinct from indignation, which is a virtuous and ultimately comforting anger – a reassuring stance that is the stuff of which clear consciences are made. Indignation is a noisy and (self-)righteous affair; we denounce the injustice at the top of our voices and willingly make something of a spectacle of ourselves. Shame, by contrast, is mute because it is a form of suffering, a terrible disconnection between the scale of the outrage and the sense of one's own impotence. In Levi's account, shame is the common ground between the exhausted prisoners and the stunned Russian soldiers, paralysed by the spectacle of these human beings in tatters who are not even capable of greeting them or smiling at them for bringing liberation and salvation. Shame sketches out the contours, still vague but insistent, of a political community.

I see a similar process occurring in the mind of James Baldwin when he sees a Douglas Martin photograph in Paris featuring Dorothy Counts, the first black pupil to be admitted to Harding High School. The photographer captures the teenager on her way to school surrounded by a spiteful, jeering mob of well-groomed young whites.

> That's when I saw the photograph. Facing us, on every newspaper kiosk on that wide, tree-shaded boulevard in Paris were photographs of fifteen-year-old Dorothy Counts being reviled and spat upon by the mob as she was making her way to school in Charlotte, North Carolina. There was unutterable pride, tension, and anguish in that girl's face as she approached the halls of learning, with history, jeering, at her back. It made me furious, it filled me with both hatred and pity. And it made me ashamed. Some one of us should have been there with her![11]

We should have been there with her. Shame is a marker of solidarity. Anger and hatred in the face of the idiocy of the world and the cruelty of the privileged, but also a simmering anger with oneself: What did I do to prevent this? Nothing.

Greek philosophers located the root of shame in the *thumos* (heart), which should be thought of not in the sentimental but in the dynamic sense of 'working your heart out': It is an ardour, an energy for transforming oneself and the world, a fuel of existence. In anchoring it there, the Greeks established it as a companion to anger, though we should bear in mind that for Aristotle anger never denoted irrational behaviour, excessive passion or uncontrollable impulses. It is worth quoting his definition again, this time in full:

> Let us then define anger as a longing, accompanied by pain (*orexis meta lupês*), for a manifest revenge (*timôrias phainomenês*) for a manifest slight (*phainomenên oligôrian*) affecting a man himself or one of his friends, when such a slight is undeserved.[12]

There thus exists a sadness in anger (*meta lupês*) that bears the same hue as shame. One *suffers* the reductive judgement, the humiliating put-down, the mortifying setback. And anger immediately gives rise to a desire for revenge: I am not what you designate me to be. Contempt is a denial of justice (in that it is undeserved) and anger conveys an individual's spirited revolt against being pigeonholed in this way. I will *not* be reduced to this caricature; I am not the contemptible cliché that you paint me to be.

What initially is experienced as painful frustration and debilitating rage can (unless it persists as violence turned back on oneself) be purified and sublimated into directed, collective political anger.

Shame can be revolutionary not only because it is associated with our anger against the world and ourselves but also because it is powered by the imagination. We need imagination to be ashamed. In its most destructive, sterile, distressing and paranoid form, the imagination projects me as an object of shame in the eyes of others: How they must look down on me right now, or worse still pity me! I can hear their derisive laughter and hateful mockery, and I can see the disgust on their faces. I want to retreat into silence and cut myself off from everyone. Confronting other people, or simply being in their presence, would be a calamity. Imagination condemns me to solitude when it is placed in the service of sadness.

But this is a case of a misfiring imagination – it means that my shame has not been sufficiently inflamed by anger. A properly functioning imagination rises ardently to the occasion, redrawing identity boundaries, inventing new identities and sources of solidarity and channelling rage. It has the power to reconfigure and project: No, I am not the pathetic person you think I am, I am worth so much more than your disdain. The imagination is dynamic and shifts my frame of reference. Rousseau pointed out that pity implies a form of movement since it involves stepping outside ourselves and into another's shoes ('It is not in ourselves, it is in him that we suffer').[13] In the same vein, the spectacle of somebody being humiliated, pathetically attempting not to lose face or inexorably becoming an object of ridicule does not leave me unscathed: I feel ashamed and bad for that person because my imagination has transported me into the panicked heart of their suffering.

To imagine is to step outside myself and expand my horizons and perspectives. When Gilles Deleuze considers Primo Levi's phrase 'being ashamed of being a man', he reaches not for examples of shame endured but for those moments when we feel ashamed *for others*. He mentions the pathetic remarks of a racist taxi driver and feels ashamed for him, which is to say that he shifts his perspective to that of a resentful, frustrated man poisoned by hatred, and he duly feels panicked by the experience. This shift is the imagination at work.

What the imagination does first and foremost is to strip reality of the consent habitually associated with it. When asked to define reality, people will generally speak of such things as materialism, coherence or efficient causation, but, in so doing, they tend to overlook an inconspicuous little element that is nevertheless of crucial importance: implicit consent. When people say that a thing or a situation is *real*, we need to pay attention to the little voice whispering in the background: 'Listen, do not tire yourself out. Stop resisting; it is just reality and we have to resign ourselves to it, comply with it, put up with it and subscribe to it. Stop rebelling.' On the lips of the powerful, pronounced with a hypocritical sigh and a feigned weariness but genuine self-importance ('What can you do? That's how things are …'), what reality means is specifically that which has to be accepted. After all, social injustice and unfair discrimination have always existed. Do your job, earn your pittance, keep your head down, count yourself lucky and knuckle down to the dirty work in the knowledge that if you don't do it, somebody else will.

But then the power of the imagination kicks in and kicks against this state of affairs: Just because a thing is real does not mean we have to accept it. The true banality of evil is not (or not only) the 'absence of thinking', as Hannah Arendt asserted. This would be to credit thinking with too much power and influence over our lives and decisions. The root of the banality of evil is a lack of imagination: My inability to put myself in the other guy's shoes or to envisage other possible worlds. And indeed, the entire social system and mass culture are designed to *discourage* the exercising of the imagination.

Immediately after writing 'shame is a revolution in itself', Marx continues: 'And if a whole nation were to feel ashamed it would be like a lion recoiling in order to spring.'[14] Everything is here: the rage, the animal possibilities, the collective dimension and the concomitant transformation of oneself and the world. Shame is a painful fluctuation between sadness and anger that can have two outcomes: It can lead us down a cold and dark path that disfigures us and ends in solitary resignation, or a fiery and luminous path that transfigures us and fuels collective anger.

The Paris Commune was the explosion of shame-cum-anger in the wake of the crushing defeat at the hands of the Prussians. 'The Commune was to be the avenger of all the shame they had suffered, the liberator, coming with fire and sword to purify and punish.'[15]

For Salman Rushdie, the two principal roots of violence are shame and shamelessness.[16] And they are not the same kind of violence.

Notes

Foreword

1 J.-J. Rousseau, *The Confessions*, Book II, trans. J. M. Cohen, Penguin Classics, 1953. See P. Hochart's brilliantly insightful analysis, 'L'espace intime', in C. Habib, *La Pudeur: la réserve et le trouble*, Autrement, 1992, 188–200.

2 S. Tisseron, *La Honte. Psychanalyse d'un lien social*, Dunod, 2020, 4th edition. V. de Gaulejac, *Les Sources de la honte*, Seuil, 2015, 2nd edition. D. Eribon, *Une morale du minoritaire*, Flammarion, 2015. C. Janin, *La Honte, ses figures et ses destins*, PUF, 2007. J.-P. Martin, *La Honte. Réflexions sur la littérature*, Gallimard, 'Folio essais', 2017. R. Ogien, *La honte est-elle immorale?*, Bayard, 2002.

3 F. Bon, *Daewoo*, Fayard, 2004.

4 J. Ziegler, *Lesbos. La honte de l'Europe*, Seuil, 2020.

5 B. Cyrulnik, *Mourir de dire: La honte*, Odile Jacob, 2012.

6 See, for example, E. Bidaud, C. Trono, *Il n'y a plus de honte dans la culture*, Penta, 2010.

7 A. Finkielkraut, G. Hanus, 'Il y a quelque chose à dire en faveur de la honte', in *Cahiers d'études lévinassiennes* 7, 2008.

8 F. Gros, *Disobey! A Philosophy of Resistance*, trans. David Fernbach, Verso, 2020.

9 P. Levi, *The Drowned and the Saved*, trans. Raymond Rosenthal, Simon & Schuster Paperbacks, 2017.

10   To emphasise the decentring effect that the imagination can bring about in relation to pity (shame and pity being the two great interpersonal emotions dependent on the imagination), Rousseau wrote in his posthumously published *Essay on the Origin of Languages* (1781): 'We suffer only as much as we judge he suffers; it is not in ourselves, it is in him that we suffer.' J.-J. Rousseau, *Essay on the Origin of Languages and Writings Related to Music*, trans. John T. Scott, University Press of New England, 1998, 306.

11   In his hard-hitting books that deliberately stretch the boundaries of literature, shame is a central concern of the novelist Édouard Louis, but not merely as a neatly demarcated theme – he uses it as a subjective resource, a perspective *from which* to write (see the interview with C. Devarrieux in *Libération*, 4 May 2018).

1. A Bad Reputation

1   On this point, see J. G. Peristiany (ed.), *Honour and Shame: The Values of Mediterranean Society*, University of Chicago Press, 1966; C. Cassar, *Honour and Shame in the Mediterranean*, Midsea Books, 2003.

2   See the conclusion of J. Pitt-Rivers, *The Fate of Shechem or the Politics of Sex: Essays in the Anthropology of the Mediterranean*, Cambridge University Press, 1977.

3   F. H. Stewart, 'Honor', in *L'Homme* 37 (143), July–September 1997.

4   On this opposition (and its connection with shame), see F. Tricaud, *L'Accusation*, Dalloz, 1977.

5   Regarding this mechanism, the most compelling analysis remains the essay 'Le système vindicatoire' in R. Verdier (ed.), *La Vengeance*, Cujas, 1980.

6   S. Obaid-Chinoy, *A Girl in the River: The Price of Forgiveness*, Oscar for best documentary short film, 2016.

7   J. Conrad, *Lord Jim*, Oxford University Press, 2008. See J.-L. Donnet's analysis, '*Lord Jim ou la honte de vivre*', in *L'Humour et la Honte*, PUF, 2008.

2. Societies Without Honour?

1   R. Descartes, *Passions of the Soul*, Art 205, 57, trans. Jonathan Bennett, 2017.

2   B. Spinoza, *Short Treatise on God, Man, and His Well-Being*, 96, trans. A. Wolf, Russell & Russell, 1963.

3   For the distinction between 'shame cultures' and 'guilt cultures', see the groundbreaking insights of R. Benedict in *The Chrysanthemum and the Sword: Patterns of Japanese Culture*, Houghton Mifflin, 1946, which have been built on by E. R. Dodds in *The Greeks and the Irrational*, University of California Press, 1951, and B. Williams in *Shame and Necessity*, University of California Press, 1993.

4   Saint Augustine, *The City of God, Book I*, chapter XIX, trans. Marcus Dods, Random House, 1950.

5   Of the many dozens of authors who could be cited, see, for example, L. Dumont, *From Mandeville to Marx: The Genesis and Triumph of Economic Ideology*, University of Chicago Press, 1977, and C. Tilly, *Coercion, Capital, and European States, AD 990–1990*, Blackwell, 1990.

6   M. Foucault, *Abnormal: Lectures at the Collège de France, 1974–1975*, trans. Graham Burchell, Picador, 2004.

7   See the collection of *lettres de cachet* compiled by M. Foucault and A. Farge in *Disorderly Families: Infamous Letters from the Bastille Archives*, trans. Thomas Scott-Railton, University of Minnesota Press, 2016.

8   See B. E. Harcourt, *Exposed: Desire and Disobedience in the Digital Age*, Harvard University Press, 2015.

9   J. Ronson, *So You've Been Publicly Shamed*, Macmillan, 2015.

3. Social Disdain

1   Act II, Scene 8 in E. Rostand, *L'Aiglon*, 1900.

2   A. Ernaux, *Cleaned Out*, trans. Carol Saunders, Dalkey Archive Press, 1990, 39.

3   A. Ernaux, *Retour à Yvetot*, Mauconduit, 2013, 22.

4   Ibid.

5   A. Ernaux, *A Woman's Story*, trans. Tanya Leslie, Four Walls Eight Windows, 1991.

6   F. Fanon, 'The Lived Experience of the Black Man' in *Black Skin, White Masks*, trans. Richard Philcox, Grove Press, 2008, 89.

7   D. Eribon, *Returning to Reims*, trans. Michael Lucey, Semiotext(e), 2013.

8   J. London, *Martin Eden*, Penguin Books, 1980, 309.

9   Translator's note (TN): *Le Dîner de cons* is a very successful film released in 1998 that has entered French popular culture. A group of sophisticated Parisians invite unsuspecting 'idiots' (*cons*) to weekly dinner parties and make fun of them.

10 R. Hoggart, *The Uses of Literacy*, Chatto and Windus, 1957.

11 G. Mordillat, *Vive la sociale!*, Points, 2005.

12 A. Ernaux, *A Man's Place*, trans. Tanya Leslie, Four Walls Eight Windows, 1992, 80.

13 Epictetus, 'On the Cynic Calling' in *The Discourses of Epictetus*, trans. Robin Hard, J. M. Dent, 1995, 194.

14 de Gaulejac, *Les Sources de la honte*; C. Dejours, *Souffrance en France. La banalisation de l'injustice sociale*, Seuil, 2009.

15 In V. Hugo, *Les Châtiments*, 1853.

16 Aristotle, *Rhetoric*, Book II, 1378b.

17 Annie Ernaux, '"I wanted to avenge my race"', in the weekly news and culture magazine *Le Nouvel Obs* (since renamed *L'Obs*), December 2011. [TN: She is using the word *race* here to refer to her social class, i.e., the working class.]

18 A. Camus, *The First Man*, trans. David Hapgood, Chivers Press, 1996, 224.

4. A Ghost Story

1   M. de Montaigne, *The Complete Essays*, Penguin 1993, 380.

2   'It is in its primary structure shame before somebody.' J.-P. Sartre, *Being and Nothingness*, trans. Hazel E. Barnes, Philosophical Library, 1956, 221.

3   V. Hugo, 'La Conscience', in *La Légende des siècles* (1859–1877).

4   V. Hugo, 'Man's Conscience Is God Thinking', in the preface to *Les Châtiments*, 1853.

5   I. Kant, *The Metaphysics of Morals*, *The Doctrine of Virtue*, I, 13, trans. Mary Gregor, Cambridge University Press, 1996, 189.

6   The imaginary and symbolic, along with the real, are concepts within the psychoanalytical system of Jacques Lacan.

7   First observed, described and theorised by P.-C. Racamier in 1986.

8   The term was coined by H. Kohut (see 'Thoughts on Narcissism and Narcissistic Rage', in *Psychoanalytic Study of the Child* 27, 1972, 360–401).

9   S. Freud, 'On Narcissism: An Introduction', in *The Freud Reader*, Peter Gay (ed.), W. W. Norton, 1989, 556.

10   B. Friedan, *The Feminine Mystique*, 1963.

11   For further details, see D. Toutenu, D. Settelen, *L'Affaire Romand. Le narcissisme criminel*, L'Harmattan, 2003.

12   E. Carrère, *The Adversary: A True Story of Murder and Deception*, trans. Linda Coverdale, Metropolitan Books, 2000, 7, 14.

13   F. Kafka, *The Trial*, trans. Willa and Edwin Muir, Schocken Books, 1995, 229.

14   Ibid.

15   P. Levi, in *Il manifesto*, 5 May 1983.

16   F. Kafka, *The Diaries of Franz Kafka*, M. Brod (ed.), trans. Joseph Kresh, 387 (extract from 1917), Penguin Books, 1949.

5. Melancholy

1   É. Zola, *L'Assommoir*, 1877.

2   S. Freud, Preface to the German edition of J. G. Bourke, *Scatalogic Rites of All Nations*, Martino Fine Books, 2009.

3   L. Binswanger, 'The Case of Ellen West' in R. May, E. Angel, H. F. Ellenberger (eds), *Existence: A New Dimension in Psychiatry and Psychology*, trans. Dr Werner Mendel and Dr Joseph Lyons, Basic Books, 1958, 237–364.

4   M. Scheler, 'Shame and Feelings of Modesty' in *Person and Self-Value, Three Essays*, trans. Manfred Frings, Martinus Nijhoff Publishers, 1987.

5   A. Mardon, 'Honte et dégoût dans la fabrication du féminin' in *Ethnologie française* 41, 2011.

6   É. de La Boétie, *Discourse on Voluntary Servitude*, 1576.

7   F. Virgili, *La France « virile ». Des femmes tondues à la Libération*, Payot, 2019.

8   I. Hermann, *L'Instinct filial*, French trans. G. Kassai, Denoël, 1973.

9   J. Bowlby, *Attachment and Loss, Vol. 1, Attachment*, Basic Books, 1983.

10   See for example S. S. Tomkins in *Affect, Imagery, Consciousness, Vol II, The Negative Affects*, Springer, 1963.

6. The Total Social Fact

1   A. Ernaux, *A Girl's Story*, trans. Alison L. Strayer, Fitzcarraldo Editions, 2020.

2   R. Antelme, *The Human Race*, trans. Jeffrey Haight and Annie Mahler, Marlboro Press / Northwestern, 1998, 231–2.

3   J.-Y. Le Naour, *Les Soldats de la honte*, Tempus-Perrin, 2013.

4   D. Fassin, R. Rechtman, *The Empire of Trauma*, trans. Rachel Gomme, Princeton University Press, 2009.

5   This has been especially well studied by D. Scotto di Vettimo in *Vivre et survivre dans la honte. Aspects cliniques, psychopathologiques et théoriques*, PUG, 2007.

6   For the minutes of the court proceedings, see G. Halimi, *Viol. Le procès d'Aix-en-Provence*, L'Harmattan, 2012, which can be read in conjunction with J.-Y. Le Naour, C. Valenti, *Et le viol devint un crime*, Vendémiaire, 2014.

7   'Any act of sexual penetration of any nature whatsoever committed on the person of another or on the perpetrator's own person through violence, constraint, threat or deceit is a rape.'

8   L'Express, 21 December 2017 (article by E. Tôn).

9   É. Thomas, *Le Viol du silence*, Aubier, 1986.

10   See for example V. Le Goaziou, *Viol. Que fait la justice?*, Presses de Sciences Po, 2019; N. Renard, *En finir avec la culture du viol*, Les Petits Matins, 2018; D. Dussy, *Le Berceau des dominations*, Pocket, 2021; M. Salmona, *Le Livre noir des violences sexuelles*, Dunod, 2019, 2nd edition D. Sigaud, *Peau d'Âne et l'Ogre. Viol et inceste sur mineurs en France*, Albin Michel, 2021.

11   *L'Humanité*, 14 June 2017 (article by M. Barbier).

12   Brut video clip, 14 March 2020.

13   S. Freud, 'The Economic Problem of Masochism', 1924, trans. Joan Riviere, in *Freud on Women: A Reader*, W. W. Norton & Company, 1992, 285.

14   He specifies 'among the Italian Camorrista', but even so … (H. Ellis, *Analysis of the Sexual Impulse, Love and Pain, The Sexual Impulse in Women*, F. A. Davis, 1913, 80).

15   M.-T.-D. de Bienville, *Nymphomania, or, a Dissertation Concerning the Furor Uterinus. Clearly and Methodically Explaining the Beginning, Progress, and Different Causes of That Horrible Distemper*, trans. Edward Sloane Wilmot, Gala Eco Print Editions, 2018.

16 Tertullian, *De cultu feminarum* (end of the second century).

17 'Her own violence is in her charms', J.-J. Rousseau, *Émile, or, On Education*, Book V, trans. Allan Bloom, Basic Books, 1979, 358.

18 For an analysis of how rape is punished only insofar as a bastard son may complicate the passing on of an inheritance, see G. Vigarello, *A History of Rape*, trans. Jean Birrell, Polity, 2001.

19 Halimi, *Viol. Le procès d'Aix-en-Provence*.

20 'I authorize and give up my right of governing myself to this man, or to this assembly of men, on the condition that you give up your right to him, and authorize all of his actions in a like manner.' T. Hobbes, *Leviathan*, Pearson Longman, 2016, 116.

21 Ibid., chapter 20.

22 'In light of these statements, are we really to believe that they were like Monsieur Seguin's goat, who struggled all night but was eaten by the wolf in the morning?' Halimi, *Viol. Le procès d'Aix-en-Provence*, 388. [TN: The reference is to a short story by Alphonse Daudet first published in 1866.]

23 V. Despentes, *King Kong Theory*, trans. Stéphanie Benson, Serpent's Tail, 2009, 27–31.

24 Halimi, *Viol. Le procès d'Aix-en-Provence*, 330.

25 S. Ferenczi, 'Confusion of Tongues Between Adults and the Child – The Language of Tenderness and of Passion' in *Contemporary Psychoanalysis* 24:2, William Alanson White Institute, 1988.

26 E. Levinas, *On Escape*, trans. Bettina Bergo, Stanford University Press, 2003, 64. This is the pertinent phrase for our purposes. Levinas actually defines shame as an ontological revelation, which is not an avenue I wish to explore here.

27 Despentes, *King Kong Theory*, 44.

28 On this concept, see the precious insights of D. Eribon in 'La voix absente. Philosophie des états généraux', in É. Louis (ed.), *Pierre Bourdieu. L'insoumission en héritage*, PUF, 2013.

29 Despentes, *King Kong Theory*, 28.

7. The Sexual Foundations of the Republic

1 Livy, *Ab urbe condita*, Book I, 57–8. Ovid, *The Book of Days*, Book II, lines 721–852. Dionysius of Halicarnassus, *Roman Antiquities*, Book V. W. Shakespeare, 'The Rape of Lucrece', 1594. A. Obey, *Le Viol de*

Lucrèce, Nouvelles Éditions Latines, 1931. Musical treatments include G. F. Handel, *Lucreẓia*, 1709; M. Pignolet de Montéclair, *La morte di Lucretia*, 1728; B. Britten, *The Rape of Lucretia*, 1946.

2 *Three Plays of Racine*, trans. George Dillon, University of Chicago Press, 1962, 153.

3 Saint Augustine, *The City of God*, Book XIV, chapter 15, 422.

4 Livy, 'The History of Rome from Its Foundation' in *The Early History of Rome*, trans. Aubrey de Sélincourt, Penguin, 1971, Book I, chapter 58, 99.

5 For an extensive list of her possible motives, see J.-M. Chaumont, *Survivre à tout prix ?*, La Découverte, 2017.

6 The automatic nature of this sullying process is well described by Vigarello in *A History of Rape*.

7 Saint Augustine, *The City of God*, Book I, 24–5.

8 P. Veyne, 'La famille et l'amour sous le Haut-Empire romain', *Annales ESC* 1, 1978.

9 In 2014 at the Odéon-Théâtre de l'Europe in Paris, Angélica Liddell proposed a transgressive and provocative version of Lucretia that challenged these fixed political and sexual identities. It is an extreme vision centred around a scandalous equation: rape = act of love. Frantic with desire, Tarquin violently delivers Lucretia from her status as perfect woman and ideal wife: 'And this is how a rapist turned me into his lover. For of all the men around me – father, husband and friends, all of them obsessed with my virtue and slaves to their ambitions, with my still-warm blood on their knives – the only one who spoke of love, the only one who didn't speak of the fatherland, government, war or politics, the only one who opted to throw away everything for a fleeting moment of love was the rapist Tarquin', *You Are My Destiny (Lo stupro di Lucreẓia)*.

8. *Aidos*

1 F. Nietzsche, *The Gay Science*, trans. Walter Kaufmann, Vintage Books, 1974, aphorisms 273, 274, 275, 220.

2 Confucius, *The Analects*, trans. Annping Chin, Penguin, 2014, II, 3, 76.

3 Plato, *The Symposium*, trans. Christopher Gill, Penguin, 1999, 10.

4 S. Leys, quoted by C. J.-D. Javary in *Les Trois sagesses chinoises*, Albin Michel, 2010.

5   For further information on Chinese philosophy, in particular its treatment of shame, see A. Cheng, 'Vertus de la pudeur dans la Chine classique', in Habib, *La Pudeur*, 74–90.

6   Confucius, *The Analects*, 461.

7   Plato, *Protagoras*, 322d.

8   Plato, *The Symposium*, 178c–179b.

9   Ibid., 178c–d.

10 Plato, *Laws*, 647a.

11 Plato, *The Symposium*, 178d.

12 A line attributed to the Stagirite, though we cannot be sure that he actually said or wrote it (the first to cite it is Diogenes Laertius in *The Lives and Opinions of Eminent Philosophers*).

13 Plato, *The Symposium*, 216a–b.

9. Philosophy as the Great Shamer

1   Homily of 9 March 2020, popefrancishomilies.com/shame.

2   See Alcuin of York (735–804) in *De confessione peccatorum, ad Pueros S. Martini Epistola*.

3   Quoted by D. Bernard, 'La honte de vivre', in J.-L. Gaspard, *La Souffrance de l'être*, Érès, 2014, 63–76.

4   Plato, *Gorgias*, 487a–b.

5   Plato, *Sophist*, trans. Benjamin Jowett, 230 b–d.

6   Ibid.

7   Ibid.

8   J. Lacan, *L'Envers de la psychanalyse*, Seuil, 1991, 223.

10. Future Imperfect

1   Despentes, *King Kong Theory*, 39.

2   Chaumont, *Survivre à tout prix?*

3   See the chapter 'Shame' in Levi, *The Drowned and the Saved*.

4   Conceptualised by G. Agamben (in particular in *Homo Sacer – Sovereign Power and Bare Life*, trans. Daniel Heller-Roazen, Stanford University Press, 1998), the term *bare life*, which appears for the first time in Walter

Benjamin, denotes life simultaneously as merely a beating heart and something invested with a sacred dimension.

5   TN: All of these words – *survie, surhomme, sur-valeur* and *sur-savoir* – carry the *sur-* prefix in French. In English, the prefixes *sur-* and *super-* have equivalent meanings.

6   Alain, 'Propos du 13 novembre 1909' in *Propos impertinents (1906–1911)*, Mille et Une Nuits, 2002.

7   TN: The form and meaning of the English future perfect tense (I will have finished) and the French *futur antérieur* (*J'aurai fini*) are equivalent. However, the *futur antérieur* can also be used to speculate or express probabilities, where in English we would use a modal perfect. The preceding sentence, translated with 'must have been', originally read in French: *J'aurai été victime d'un inceste, j'aurai été violé.*

8   J. Lacan, *Freud's Papers on Technique 1953–1954*, trans. John Forrester, Cambridge University Press, 1988, lecture of 7 April 1954, 159. The complete phrase is: 'What we see in the return of the repressed is the effaced signal of something which only takes on its value in the future, through its symbolic realisation, its integration into the history of the subject. Literally, it will only ever be a thing which, at the given moment of its occurrence, will have been.'

9   See previous chapter, 'The Sexual Foundations of the Republic'.

10 See previous chapter, 'A Ghost Story'.

11 Levi, *The Drowned and the Saved*, 56.

12 Ibid., 57.

13 Ibid., 62.

14 Ibid., 63.

15 Ibid.

16 Levi himself in fact slides between one word and the other, for which he is unjustly criticised by G. Agamben (See 'Shame, or On the Subject' in *Remnants of Auschwitz: The Witness of the Archive*, trans. D. Heller-Roazen, Zone Books, 2002).

17 The complete phrase is: 'Living the shame of life and maintaining silence, that was the greatest accomplishment of all.' (*Liquidation*, trans. Tim Wilkinson, Alfred A. Knopf, 2004).

18 P. Levi, *The Truce: A Survivor's Journey Home from Auschwitz*, trans. Stuart Woolf, The Folio Society, 2002, 239.

11. Intersectional Shame

1   Sartre, *Being and Nothingness*, 352.
2   Ibid., 349.
3   R. Wright, *Native Son*, Harper Perennial Modern Classics, 2023.
4   P. Bergounioux, *École: mission accomplie*, Les Prairies Ordinaires, 2006, 62.
5   Bon, *Daewoo*.
6   S. Weil, 'Journal d'usine' in *La Condition ouvrière*, La République des Lettres, 2019, 133.
7   J. Baldwin, radio interview with Studs Terkel, 1961.
8   C. Lomba, *La Restructuration permanente de la condition ouvrière*, Le Croquant, 2018.
9   Preface by C. Taubira to the French translation of J. Baldwin's *The Fire Next Time* (*La prochaine fois, le feu*, Gallimard, 2018, 13). I. Boni-Claverie, *Too Black to Be French*, documentary, 2017. T. de Montaigne, *L'Assignation. Les Noirs n'existent pas*, Grasset, 2014.
10 Fanon, 'The Lived Experience of the Black Man'.
11 W. E. B. Du Bois, 'Of Our Spiritual Strivings' in *The Souls of Black Folk: Essays and Sketches*, A. C. McClurg, 1903, 2.
12 *I Am Not Your Negro*, a film on J. Baldwin citing his writings by R. Peck and also a book of the same name, Vintage Books, 2017, 107.
13 J. Baldwin, *The Fire Next Time*, Dell Publishing, 1964, 32.
14 Fanon, 'The Lived Experience of the Black Man', 96.

12. Systemic Shame

1   P. Levi, 'On Translating Kafka' in *La Stampa*, 5 June 1983, trans. Raymond Rosenthal.
2   Levi, *The Drowned and the Saved*, 65.
3   *L'Abécédaire*, a documentary made by Pierre-André Boutang featuring interviews with G. Deleuze conducted between 1988 and 1989. This quote is from the 'Resistance' segment.
4   C. Lévi-Strauss, *Tristes Tropiques*, trans. John and Doreen Weightman, Penguin Books, 1976, 542.
5   P. Levi, 'Words, Memory, Hope' in *The Voice of Memory – Interviews 1961–1987*, trans. Robert Gordon, Polity Press, 2001, 254.

6   G. Flaubert, letter to Louise Colet on 26 August 1853, in *The Selected Letters of Gustave Flaubert*, trans. Francis Steegmuller, Books for Libraries Press, 1971, 163–4.

7   G. Sand, letter to Mme Marliani, July 1848, in *Letters of George Sand*, trans. Veronica Lucas, George Routledge & Sons, 1930, 164.

8   S. Weil, *Simone Weil on Colonialism: An Ethic of the Other*, trans. J. P. Little, Rowman & Littlefield, 2003, 47–8.

9   C. Ginzburg, *Libération* newspaper, 10 October 2019.

10   Shame is a 'sort of immunisational defence', Levi, *The Drowned and the Saved*, 66.

11   Baldwin, *The Fire Next Time*, 15–16.

12   F. Dostoevsky, *Notes from Underground*, trans. Jessie Coulson, Penguin Books, 1972.

13. Revolutionary Shame

1   L. S. Senghor, *Hosties noires*, Seuil, 1956.

2   R. Depestre, *Minerai noir*, Seuil, 2019.

3   Ferenczi, 'Confusion of Tongues'.

4   When it comes to Jean Genet, in addition to J.-P. Sartre's exhaustive (and exhausting) *Saint Genet – Actor And Martyr*, trans. Bernard Frechtman, University of Minnesota Press, 2012, precious insights can be gleaned from Eribon in *Une Morale du minoritaire*, and from C. Vettier's fine article 'Honte et transparence: écrire sa honte, de Rousseau à Genet' in *SELF XX-XXI – Journée d'études* 'Ombres et transparences', October 2018.

5   J. Genet, *The Thief's Journal*, trans. Bernard Frechtman, Grove Press, 1987, 175.

6   Ibid.

7   Ibid.

8   Ibid.

9   Ibid.

10   Levi, *The Truce*, 22.

11   Baldwin, *I Am Not Your Negro*, 12.

12   Aristotle, *Rhetoric*, Book II, 1378b.

13   Rousseau, *Essay on the Origin of Languages*, 306. For Rousseau's most comprehensive treatment of pity, see *Emile, or On Education*, Book V, 1762.

14   K. Marx, letter to Ruge, March 1843 ('From a barge on the way to D.'), first published in *Deutsch-Französische Jahrbücher 1844*, Progress Publishers, available at the Marx Engels Archive. The full quote is: 'I can see you smile and say: what good will that do? Revolutions are not made by shame. And my answer is that shame is a revolution in itself; it really is the victory of the French Revolution over that German patriotism which defeated it in 1813. Shame is a kind of anger turned in on itself. And if a whole nation were to feel ashamed it would be like a lion recoiling in order to spring. I admit that even this shame is not yet to be found in Germany.'

15   É. Zola, *The Downfall (La Débâcle)*, trans. E. P. Robins, Mondial, 2008, 397 (translation modified).

16   'Shamelessness, shame: the roots of violence.' S. Rushdie, *Shame*, Alfred A. Knopf, 1983, 124.